W9-AOP-651

POLICE

UNDER FIRE

TED GOTTFRIED

Twenty-First Century Books
Brookfield, Connecticut

For my daughter, Valerie Gottfried, and all
the children she helps—with all my love.

Photographs courtesy of Photofest: p. 13; Impact Visuals: pp. 17 (© 1992 Anita
Bartsch), 60 (© Tom McKitterick), 63 (© Tom McKitterick), 89 (© 1993 Paul
Dix), 97 (© 1991 Robert Fox); North Wind Picture Archives: p. 22; Texas Ranger
Hall of Fame and Museum: p. 28; Liaison Agency, Inc.: pp. 36 (© Karl Gehring),
55 (© Bill Swersey); Agence France Press/Corbis-Bettmann: p. 50; AP/Wide
World Photos: p. 52; Los Angeles Times Photo, Genaro Molina: p. 72; UPI/
Corbis-Bettmann: p. 80

Published by Twenty-First Century Books
A Division of The Millbrook Press, Inc.
2 Old New Milford Road, Brookfield, Connecticut 06804

Library of Congress Cataloging-in-Publication Data
Gottfried, Ted.
Police under fire / Ted Gottfried.
p. cm. — Includes bibliographical references and index.
ISBN 0-7613-1313-3 (lib. bdg.)
1. Police—United States. 2. Police misconduct—United States. 3. Racism—
United States. 4. Minorities—Crimes against—United States. 5. Police
community relations—United States. 6. Criminal justice, Administration of—
United States. I. Title. II. Series.
HV8138.G672 1999   363.2'0973—dc21   98-55074   CIP

I am most grateful to my friend and volunteer researcher Jean Orben for her help and advice in writing this book. It would also not have been possible without the expertise in computer-building and program-running of Dan, Loraine, and Jonathan Gottfried. Many thanks to the personnel of the New York Central Research Library, the Mid-Manhattan Library, and especially the Epiphany Branch Library and the central branch of the Queensboro Public Library. Finally—with much love—I want to acknowledge the contribution of my wife, Harriet Gottfried, who, as always, read and critiqued this book.

Their help was invaluable, but any shortcomings in the work are mine alone.

—Ted Gottfried

CONTENTS

POLICE
UNDER FIRE ⟵

CHAPTER ONE
GOOD COP, BAD COP

"I'll promote the men who kick these gorillas around and bring them in, and I'll demote any policemen who are friendly with gangsters."[1]

—Lewis J. Valentine,
New York City Police
Commissioner (1934–1945)

When you see a uniformed police officer, what is your reaction? Do you feel reassured, protected, and safe? Or do you feel uneasy, threatened, and in danger? Whatever your response, it may have as much to do with who you are as it does with the officer.

It may depend on whether you're rich or poor, white or a member of a minority group, straight or gay, a natural-born citizen or an immigrant, an adolescent or an adult, whether you live in a rural area or the suburbs or the inner city, and even, in some cases, whether you're male or female. The emotions the police arouse at first sight hinge on a variety of factors that often—if not always—have little to do with the officers themselves. People respond to their own image of the police, and while that may be based on personal experience, it may also stem from exposure to the six o'clock news, the daily paper, TV cop shows, and the movies.

CRACKDOWNS: PRO AND CON

Individual citizens may praise the police or curse them, but when it comes to the public as a whole, the polls reveal mixed and sometimes contradictory attitudes. They give police credit for a 10 percent nationwide drop in violent crime in 1996. They praise the police for a reduction in the homicide rate from "10.5 murders per 100,000 persons in 1993 to eight in 1995 (the most recent national data available from the FBI) and [which] probably will be far lower for 1996 and 1997."[2]

The public tends to agree with President Bill Clinton and many mayors that "community policing has led to the decline [in crime]."[3] In general, people approve the police campaigns in many cities to enforce so-called quality-of-life laws strictly. They agree that strict policing of such activities as panhandling, public use of boom boxes, selling liquor to minors, and others contributes to the reduction of more serious crimes.

Some of the recent innovations in policing, however, meet with public disapproval. Cracking down on jaywalkers and issuing them tickets has not proved popular. Surveillance cameras in parks frequented by drug dealers have met with protests by ordinary citizens who visit the parks. Massive drug sweeps through poor neighborhoods and housing projects have outraged many residents.

It is not just those who are immediately affected who object to some of these innovations. Many other people see such police crackdowns as a threat to the rights of or-

Popular television police dramas lend a certain mystique to police work and culture, and influence how many people view the police, whether negatively or positively. Actors Dennis Franz and Rick Schroder are pictured here during the 1998-1999 season of NYPD Blue.

dinary citizens. At the same time, most people are aware that these actions are the result of orders from above—usually originating at the political level with appointed officials—and don't blame the rank-and-file officers for them. In general, they give the police high marks for crime prevention and crime control. That is a turnaround from a few years back when crime was the number one concern of most Americans.

NEGATIVE IMAGES

On the other hand, there is a widespread perception that the police are often more brutal than they have to be and that too often they are completely out of hand. Incidents like the beating of Rodney King in Los Angeles on March 3, 1991, and the alleged torture of Abner Louima in New York City in 1997 reinforce this view. Many people believe that the use of excessive force is part of police training, culture, and tradition. This may not be fair or true, but the perception is there.

So, too, is the opinion that officers tend to be trigger-happy. It seems that not a day goes by in one part of the country or another without a police officer shooting someone unnecessarily. Sometimes the victim is an innocent bystander, or a wrongful suspect. Sometimes it is a guilty perpetrator who is shot before he or she can surrender. Sometimes the shooting does grave damage; sometimes it is fatal.

The pictures of beatings and shootings on the six o'clock news are hard to get past. The images are powerful. Is it any wonder that they become part of our vision of police in general?

But these images present only a limited view of the police. There are more than 604,000 law-enforcement officers in the United States, and the majority of them have never had occasion to fire their guns. The great majority of police in our country have never brutalized nor shot anyone.

ALL THINGS TO ALL PEOPLE

Those officers who have used their weapons may have had good reason to feel threatened. According to the Federal Bureau of Investigation (FBI), "sixty-four law-enforcement officers around the country were murdered in the line of duty last year [1997], up from fifty-six the previous year."[4] For the police, firing first is sometimes a simple matter of self-preservation.

Both the use of force and the use of firearms are viewed by many officers as complying with the public demand to "get tough on crime." But it seems that when they do, the public criticizes them and tells them to "get back in touch with the communities they serve."[5] It is a mixed message in a job that, by its very nature, requires a variety of skills.

On any given day the cop on the beat—whether on foot or in a patrol car—may be called on to deal with domestic disputes, thieves who may be armed, muggers, people who are drunk or high on drugs, rape victims or victims of other crimes, crowd control or riot control, sick people requiring help, drug dealers, racial violence, fires or explosions, speed chases, auto accidents, traffic control, and breaking the news to the families of accident or crime victims. He or she has to be both sensitive and tough, have the skill to arbitrate a quarrel and command the respect to settle it firmly, possess the good judgment to recognize when the public good is more important than apprehending a criminal, be restrained when necessary, tactful always, and thick-skinned enough not to escalate a situation when a lack of respect raises his or her adrenalin level. No officer can fulfill all of these requirements all of the time. The impressive thing is how many officers meet them so much of the time.

CHARGES OF RACISM

An additional burden has been put on police with the growth of juvenile crime. According to U.S. Attorney General Janet Reno, "Teenage crime will double by the year 2010." For those between the ages of fourteen and seventeen, "the murder rate alone rose 165 percent from 1985 to 1993."[6] Much of this crime occurs in poor areas densely populated by minorities.

Community policing—particularly foot patrolling—is effective in lowering crime in such areas. However, stop-and-frisk incidents involving youths who may or may not be gang members have aroused resentment among both young people and adults. In inner cities the police are often viewed as whites from the suburbs who behave as an occupying force.

Efforts to recruit more nonwhite officers for these areas are criticized as too little, too late. Police departments try to stress sensitivity toward nonwhites, gays, domestic-abuse victims and others, but the attitudes of officers are sometimes no easier to change than those of many citizens in the community at large. When those sentiments are put into action, the result can be racist violence.

JUDGING POLICE MISCONDUCT

Police review boards are in place to deal with incidents of bigotry, brutality, and wrongful death. However, many review boards are tied in with their police departments, and most charges against officers are dismissed. Attempts to establish independent civilian complaint review boards have usually been successfully opposed by police officials and rank-and-file unions.

Many police departments use community policing in an effort to reduce street crime and reinforce the cooperative efforts and mutual trust between the police and the people of a neighborhood. These New York City officers use bikes on their patrols.

Some of those officials, and some of those unions, have made headlines with corruption scandals. Chiefs of police, high-ranking officers, and entire precincts have been involved. Police work puts officers in close touch with criminals and the temptation to profit by the contact is ever present. The record shows, however, that most police officers in the United States don't give in to the temptation.

The individual officer may be a good cop or a bad cop. Most are good at their jobs; some aren't. As you read about the misconduct in the chapters that follow, a good idea would be to judge the police as individuals, and to judge them with sympathy and understanding—as you would want to be judged by them.

CHAPTER TWO
THE ENFORCERS OF THE LAW

"Despite many continuing charges of police corruption and brutality, there is little doubt that the policeman of today is far superior, professionally and morally, to his counterpart of earlier years."[1]
—The Encyclopedia of American Crime

Sensational reports by the media of police brutality, racism, and corruption have promoted a skeptical attitude towards police reform. Yet despite the bad apples among them, American law-enforcement officers today are far more humane, honest, and fair-minded than those who came before them. Police forces may still have serious flaws, but over the years there have been determined—and in many ways successful—efforts to clean up their act.

THE COLONIAL CONSTABLES
From the beginning, when so-called constables were appointed to keep order in the colonies that one day would

join together to create the United States of America, there were problems of dishonesty, cruelty, and bigotry among them. First the Dutch, and then the British governors of the colonies, assigned large landowners, usually political cronies, to keep order. In addition, one of their main duties was to collect taxes.

The constables were paid 10 percent of all they collected. There was much grumbling among ordinary people that while the constables were cracking down on honest taxpayers, highwaymen and other criminals were being ignored. Indeed, some of the constables were accused of being paid a percentage of the value of the stolen goods by the thieves who stole them, as well as 10 percent of the tax money.

As the population grew, so did crime, and so did the indignation of the people toward the constables. Nevertheless, from around 1608 to 1783, when the American Revolution brought an end to colonial governors and the colonial appointment of constables, the system prevailed throughout most of the colonies. Eventually, in reaction to the widespread corruption of the constables, additional methods of policing were introduced in some of the larger cities and other crime-ridden areas.

THE NIGHT WATCH AND THE LEATHERHEADS

In the 1630s the recently settled community of Boston introduced the first night watch, so-called because it patrolled during the hours between dusk and dawn when strong-arm thieves known as "jackrollers" prowled the streets and tavern brawls were most likely to disturb the peace. The first night watch consisted of a military officer and six soldiers. Later it was reorganized and expanded to consist of civilians appointed by the local colonial government. Again the favoritism involved in the appointments gave rise to rumors of corruption among the members of the night watch.

Philadelphia and New Amsterdam (now New York City) followed Boston's example and set up night watches. People on a night watch were armed with noisy rattles, on the theory that establishing a conspicuous presence in the community would deter crime (a principle that has been revived in some American cities). These patrols came to be known as *ratelwacht* (Dutch for rattlewatch).

Some communities hired day patrols in addition to night watches. In New York City, after the British replaced the Dutch as colonial rulers, the law enforcers were outfitted with heavy leather helmets to protect them in street fights and encounters with violent criminals. They occupied sentry boxes, which were spaced out around the city. Soon there were protests that the "leatherheads" were spending too much time snoozing in their coops rather than doing their jobs.

By 1762, New York City news journals were hinting that the appointment of leatherheads was too often a form of political payola. They were reporting that "various attempts to rob, and so many robberies actually committed" during both "day and night" made it "hazardous for any person to walk" in the city streets.[2] Was this due to police negligence, one New York journal wondered, or collaboration between leatherheads and criminals?

LYNCH LAW

In rural areas in the eighteenth century a different kind of law-enforcement issue was becoming a problem. With no official government agency to deal with crime and violence in what was still wilderness country, honest folk organized to establish law and order. Today we call that sort of action "vigilantism." It began with a band of civilian

This drawing shows a colonial night watchman on his rounds. Its original caption reads: "Twelve o'clock, and a pleasant morning!"

crime-fighters selected and organized by Colonel William Lynch of Pittsylvania County, Virginia.

On September 22, 1780, the group issued a manifesto declaring that "upon hearing or having sufficient reason to believe that any species of villainy [has] been committed within our neighborhood . . . we will inflict such corporeal punishment . . . as to us shall seem adequate to the crime committed or the damage sustained. . . ."[3]

In practice this meant whipping the accused criminal until he or she confessed to the crime. Once a confession had been obtained, hanging was the usual punishment. However, Lynch and his followers were squeamish about carrying out the sentence themselves. An observer described how they dealt with their qualms.

> The person . . . was placed on a horse with his hands tied behind him and a rope about his neck which was fastened to the limb of a tree over his head. In this situation the person was left and when the horse in pursuit of food or any other cause moved from his position the unfortunate person was left suspended by the neck—this was called "aiding the civil authority."[4]

Hanging a person without due process of law came to be known as lynching. Such executions were the most extreme examples of what happens when people take the law into their own hands. What had started in Virginia as an attempt to establish law and order paved the way for the mob rule and many lynchings of African-Americans in the South during a later period.

STREET GANGS AND CROWD CONTROL

Meanwhile, another problem was appearing in some cities. Street gangs, usually criminal, sometimes bigoted and/or racist, were becoming active. Local journals in Philadelphia frequently published news stories about "those nocturnal Sons of Violence,"[5] a gang that beat, robbed, and often murdered their victims after nightfall. Gang activity presented law-enforcement officers with a new and different kind of problem, one for which they had no preparation or training. Soon it was being whispered—unfairly in some, but not all, cases—that the night watches had reached an accommodation with some of the gangs and were profiting by it.

The threat of organized criminal gangs was overshadowed in the days leading up to the American Revolution by discontented citizens gathering in crowds, which increasingly turned to violence. A common response to what was viewed as unfair taxation by England was rock throwing and the destruction of property. (The most famous such incident was the Boston Tea Party, in which boatloads of tea were dumped into Boston Harbor by citizens protesting the British tax on it.)

Such actions met with a variety of responses by those nonmilitary officers charged with keeping the peace. Some, sympathizing with the crowds flouting British authority, simply ignored the disturbances. In effect, they did not do their sworn duty to uphold the law.

Others, loyal to the colonial governments that had appointed them, restored order with clubs and, sometimes, muskets. Anti-British constables could be equally ruthless in their dealings with those loyal to the crown. Such actions introduced the principle of the use of maximum force in crowd control still practiced by American police. Over the years, many would protest maximum force as police brutality.

POLITICS AS USUAL

The quality of law enforcement did not noticeably improve with the end of the American Revolution. Most of the colonial night watch and leatherhead officers were fired, but those who replaced them were not any less brutal nor any more honest than the old guard. Also, with the arrival of German and then Irish immigrants, many of them Catholic, ethnic and religious bigotry became an obstacle to fairness in urban policing.

The *Encyclopedia of American Crime* describes the police of the early republic as "a ragtag, motley crowd. Law-enforcement jobs were given on a strictly political basis, and officers usually served only a one-year term and could then be fired at whim by local aldermen. No training was given to them and they usually had no uniforms . . . These policemen were, at best, only marginally more successful than their predecessors . . . "[6]

Such officers were no match for the riots that swept through city after city in the United States during the 1830s. Protestants fought Catholics. Recent German and Irish immigrants fought second- and third-generation English and Dutch Americans. The poor rioted for food, raided warehouses, and vandalized stores. Whatever the cause of the riots, criminals profited by large-scale theft made possible by the confusion.

Every local election seemed to provide an excuse for rioting. In New York City, the Journeymen's Riot of 1834 was sparked by the question of slavery. An "eight-day rampage directed against . . . prominent abolitionists . . . as well as the homes of black residents, revealed the imperiled existence of free blacks in New York. . . . In response . . . black leaders formed the Committee of Vigilance," an answer to police inability, or unwillingness, to protect black residents.[7]

POLICE VS. POLICE

Police incompetence, bigotry, and corruption brought demands for reform in many cities. But it was not until the 1850s that police departments began to be reorganized effectively. Boston led the way by creating an efficient and disciplined police organization that followed the principles laid down by the British police reformer Robert Peel. In keeping with Peel's teachings, Boston established a system of record-keeping and communication by police-whistle signals.

Similar attempts at reform in New York City failed. In 1853 the New York State legislature created the Municipal Police to serve the city. Within four years this force had become so undisciplined and lawless that the legislature tried to abolish it. However, the Municipals provided muscle for the corrupt administration of New York City Mayor Fernando Wood, and he refused to disband them.

The legislature then created the Metropolitan Police to replace the Municipals. A state Supreme Court ruling backed up the action, and when the mayor defied it, Captain George W. Walling of the Metropolitan Police was sent to arrest him. Captain Walling was met by 300 Municipals inside City Hall. They tossed him into the street.

In response, a troop of 50 Metropolitan Police in uniforms consisting of stovepipe hats and frock coats marched on City Hall. The Municipals met them on the steps, and the battle was fought both outside and inside the building. Some 52 policemen were injured and in the end the Metropolitans retreated.

The legislature called out the National Guard. A platoon of infantry with fixed bayonets seized City Hall. Mayor Wood was arrested, but that was not the end of the rivalry. Throughout the summer of 1853 the Metropolitan Police and the Municipal Police fought pitched battles on the streets of New York while criminals had a field day. Purses were snatched, and people were mugged in broad daylight, while rival officers attacked each other with clubs to determine who had jurisdiction over the crimes being committed.

When an arrest was made by one force, aldermen, magistrates, and officials favoring the rival group would quickly arrange to have the prisoner released. Arrests rarely resulted in convictions, and often not even in prosecution. Finally public outrage became so great that Mayor Wood abolished the Municipal Police. The Metropolitan Police became the official force of New York City and order was restored—at least for a while.

FRONTIER LEGENDS

In other American cities during the 1850s and the Civil War years, there were no municipal police forces. State troopers maintained law and order in Baltimore, St. Louis, Kansas City, Detroit, Cleveland, and Chicago. After the war, however, local police forces were installed in these and other cities.

In the frontier west, though, law enforcement was a catch-as-catch-can proposition. As far back as 1826 the Texas Rangers had been created to patrol the vast ranges of that territory. An unruly group, which often brutalized prisoners and illegally pursued suspects deep into Mexican territory, they were disbanded following the Civil War.

However, the Texas Rangers were reestablished in 1874. For the next forty-five years they "consistently violated the civil rights of individuals and groups, killed unnecessarily while making arrests, and murdered prisoners." In 1919 a state House-Senate committee concluded that the Rangers were "antiblack, anti-Chicano, and antilabor."[8] Some reforms were instituted, and the Texas Rangers have continued to police rural areas through modern times.

In many frontier communities during the latter part of the nineteenth century, the law was enforced by local sheriffs and their deputies and posses. Many of the most famous among these lawmen had formerly been criminals.

A notorious bunch, the Texas Rangers policed the western frontier in the 1800s, quite often with violence and no regard for civil rights. Pictured here is the Company D Frontier Battalion in 1888.

Some would become criminals again after they gave up their badges.

Legends are numerous about such figures as Wyatt Earp, Pat Garrett, Bat Masterson, and Wild Bill Hickock, all of whom were as likely to bend the law as enforce it. In places like Dodge City, Virginia City, and Tombstone, payoffs from gambling halls and houses of prostitution might be ignored if the sheriff was able to hold down the violence and the killings.

URBAN RIOTS

The sheriffs were more successful in reducing mayhem than were many police departments in larger cities. In Los Angeles in October 1871, white citizens rampaged through Chinatown and killed 20 to 25 people. Police—probably racist themselves—were either unable or unwilling to protect the scores of Chinese Americans and Chinese immigrants who were beaten and slain in the riot.

In Cincinnati in 1884, citizens became outraged by corruption involving police and the courts. Criminals—even murderers—routinely escaped arrest and punishment. When the charges against two murderers were reduced to manslaughter with light sentences sure to follow, a mob stormed the jail and lynched them.

Violence continued over the following days. The jail was attacked, and the courthouse was set ablaze. The mob ran amok in the streets with much of their fury directed toward police officers. Finally, soldiers were brought in to restore order. By then 45 people had been killed and 138 more badly injured. In the end, however, corruption returned to Cincinnati, and for many years the police were a part of it.

THE ROOSEVELT REFORMS

Graft and corruption had also made a comeback with the police force of New York City by the 1890s. Chief of Police Big Bill Dewey and Chief Inspector Alexander S. Williams ran a department where promotion depended on cooperating with the rackets that bribed police to look the other way. These rackets included squeezing money from small shopkeepers and saloons for protection against violence, the resale of stolen goods, illegal gambling clubs, streetwalkers and high-priced brothels, and even the defrauding of Wall Street investors. Rare was the officer who didn't cut himself a piece of the payoff pie before the major slice found its way to Dewey and Williamson.

In 1895 this pair met their nemesis, and conditions began to improve for the New York City police. In that year future president Theodore Roosevelt began his three-year term as police commissioner. He zeroed in on the politically protected operations of Dewey and Williams and drove the pair out of their jobs.

Roosevelt then began reforming a department that seemed corrupt from top to bottom. When he caught officers of any rank taking bribes or protecting criminals, they were instantly dismissed. He instituted a training program for the recruits who replaced them. He enforced a policy of promotion based on merit. Widely copied in cities around the country, his programs introduced the idea of professionalism to police work. This encouraged officers to view their jobs as a form of service rather than an opportunity to profit from corruption.

A KEY SHIFT IN EMPHASIS
Professionalism didn't banish corruption, however. Neither did it solve problems of brutality and racism. What it did accomplish was create certain official standards for twentieth-century police behavior, which the majority of officers followed and a small minority violated at risk of punishment.

The balance had shifted significantly. Professionalism brought respect for officers from the general public. Now police misbehavior was scandal for media coverage rather than departmental policy visited on a defenseless public. Twentieth-century officers would not be perfect, but as a whole they would be much more principled than those who came before them.

who took the examination to join the Suffolk County Police Department in 1996, "as many as 700 . . . gained an unfair edge, mostly from illegal coaching in classes given by a police sergeant who had stolen some of the answers."[5] The grand jury investigation had been the result of complaints from African-American applicants, who charged cheating and favoritism in the hiring of Suffolk County police officers.

RESIDENCY REQUIREMENTS

In many large cities, charges of racism stem from the recruitment of white officers from the suburbs to police inner cities populated by minorities. "Race is the driving factor in the mistrust between the police and the community," according to a report issued by Michael Meyers, executive director of the New York Civil Rights Coalition, Margaret Fung, director of the Asian-American Legal Defense and Education Fund, and Norman Siegel of the New York Civil Liberties Union.[6] Many critics believe that racism common in white suburban communities and that it combines with the assertive attitudes that attract people to police work in the first place. There is a ... they say, between such attitudes and aggressiveness. When young officers from the suburbs experience culture shock of being assigned to a poor minority neighborhood—perhaps even one in which they don't speak primary language—they often react to volatile situations with a combination of fear, aggression, and bigotry. This reaction, critics say, should bar suburban candidates from a police force that often must deal with people culturally and economically diverse. A 1997–1998 ... appointed by New York's Mayor Rudolph ... agreed. It recommended "that the department require new officers to live in New York City."[7]

CHAPTER THREE
RECRUITMENT AND TRAINING

"Some experts contend that police work, with its emphasis on giving orders and establishing control, attracts many men with a propensity for . . . violence."[1]
—*New York Times* Special Report

Professionalism is still the goal for the police departments of the United States today. It is the standard that earns respect from the public. First Deputy Commissioner Patrick E. Kelleher of the City of New York Police Department (NYPD) points out that "there is no greater detriment to officer safety or successful completion of the police mission than a lack of respect for the Department or the community we serve."[2] The NYPD defines professionalism as follows:

- Acknowledging the rights and dignity of those we come in contact with.

- Acknowledging the diversity, traditions, and cultures of others.

- Being cognizant of the manner in which we speak to others.

- Being knowledgeable of our responsibilities and the extent of our authority.

- Being adept in defusing volatile situations.

- Recognizing the impact that traumatic events can have on the people we come in contact with.

- Extending respect to our colleagues, regardless of rank or position.[3]

THE SELECTION PROCESS

Critics question whether the police live up to these standards. They cite examples of rights denied, dignity offended, insensitivity to cultural differences, rudeness, excessive force, callousness, and lack of respect toward minority and women officers. Such criticisms have been directed at the police forces of Chicago, New Orleans, Philadelphia, Los Angeles, Detroit, Washington, D.C., and many other cities around the country. Most of the critics agree that the problems begin with recruitment and training.

Recruitment is highly selective in most cities. In 1994, there were 6,000 applicants to join the police force in Philadelphia. Only 300 officers were hired. There were 8,000 applicants in Fort Worth, Texas, but only 100 were accepted. Of the 57,366 would-be police officers who applied in New York City, only one in 21 was admitted to the Police Academy training program.

Hiring standards for police forces vary greatly around the country, with urban requirements usually more rigorous and small town and suburban criteria less demanding. Most applicants for city forces have to pass an in-depth

background check covering education, (ing and personal histories, as well as : ground. Metropolises like Los Angele: York may require some college educati Convictions for any crime, or dishonc the military service, will usually disq

Written examinations test me reading comprehension, map-read rules, and mathematical abilities. S measure speed, strength, and en interviews and examinations ass emotional stability, resistance to ment. Finally, thorough medic ing screening for drug and candidates with conditions th lice performance.

THE SUFFOLK COUNTY RECR

Such recruitment programs the police say they are seri against them is that they Americans, Latinos, and (the written examinations. selection process is adm nate against women.

In 1988 the Depar police department rec County, New York, Po up with "a race-neutra of minority applica force."[4]

Suffolk County force of 2,700, the ers. A 1997 grand

Officials in the New York Police Department (NYPD) oppose this requirement. They point out that there are as many complaints of brutality against officers who live in the city as against those who live in the suburbs. Police in many other cities agree. Nevertheless, community pressures are forcing them to alter recruitment procedures to hire more minorities and women.

REVISING THE TESTS

The Baltimore police force now recruits applicants from predominantly black colleges. In Los Angeles, where charges were made that written examinations were culturally loaded against minorities, the tests are given less emphasis in the selection process. The aim is to attract more inner city recruits.

Such efforts can backfire. In Washington, D.C., the City Council ordered that all new police recruits be city residents. Subsequently, Congress, which has control over Washington, threatened to withhold funds unless 1,800 new officers were hired. Washington then lowered the passing grade on its police department entrance examination from 70 percent to 50 percent in order to attract inner-city applicants. However, it was later determined that many of the new recruits "lacked the basic skills necessary to serve as competent witnesses or fill out arrest reports."[8] The 70 percent passing score had to be reinstated.

MAXIMUM FORCE

New recruits to the nation's police departments are likely to have gotten their image of police officers from television shows like *N.Y.P.D. Blue*, *Hill Street Blues*, *Brooklyn South*, or *Law and Order.* In the action sequences of these shows the police are portrayed as tough and hard-hitting. Nightsticks and gunfire control dangerous situations.

Police training has been criticized for emphasizing the use of maximum force to take control of threatening situations. But police argue that they must maintain a tough image to command authority. Are these officers-in-training in Colorado learning methods that will allow them to protect the public more effectively, or cause them to use unnecessary violence?

Miranda rights—a suspect's "right to remain silent . . . and to have a lawyer present during questioning . . ."[9]—are treated as a necessary evil and read with contempt by arresting officers. There may be episodes designed to show more sensitive aspects of police character, but in general the image is macho.

That image, say critics, is rarely modified by police training programs. For many years, the federal Law Enforcement Assistance Administration has funded sensitivity classes and seminars on the rights of the accused and on the limits of force. However, critics charge that while these programs may look good on paper, more traditional police attitudes instilled in rookies throughout their training undermine the programs' messages.

Officers have been taught, for instance, that maximum force quickly applied is the best way to establish crowd control. They have been taught powerhouse methods of breaking into homes for drug busts and other situations requiring such actions. They have spent countless hours on the shooting range honing quick response skills and developing deadly firepower. Although classes have also been offered on the need to exercise restraint, critics feel that these have too often been outweighed by a deep-seated, "macho" training tradition.

Sometimes this has included instruction on how to get around the Miranda rights of suspects. The Miranda ruling requires that questioning must stop once the person in custody has said that he or she wants a lawyer present. However, *The New York Times* has reported that in Los Angeles Police Department seminars and training videos, "officers have been told that if they continue their interrogation even though a suspect has invoked Miranda, they have little to lose and much to gain." The *Times* adds that New York "is [only] marginally more strict than California in mandating that an interrogation be stopped following a request for a lawyer."[10]

ON-THE-JOB TRAINING

"On small or rural forces, new recruits often get the bulk of their professional training on the job, working closely with an experienced officer," according to *Police Officer: The Complete Preparation Guide*, an introductory manual for recruits. "Larger departments typically require a period of formal training, often weeks or months in a police academy or other academic setting. Classroom instruction is then followed by a period of on-the-job or field training."[11]

It is during this on-the-job training period, say critics, that impressionable rookie officers are initiated into a police culture that has traditionally blocked efforts to reform it. Discussing the 1991 beating of Rodney King, the journal *Black Scholar* pointed out that there were rookies among the twenty-two Los Angeles officers who watched the four who clubbed him. Veteran officers, according to the magazine's view, regarded this as "O. J. T. (on-the-job-training)" for the rookies.[12]

The example is extreme, perhaps unfair, but veterans do routinely impress upon rookies the need to hang tough. To do their job, they say, they must maintain an image of strength. They must have the respect of those they police, or their authority will be challenged. In neighborhoods rife with drugs and violence, a cop who isn't respected can't function. Furthermore, to lose respect is to increase the risk of getting killed.

THE BLUE WALL OF SILENCE

There is more than a little justification for this view. But what it leads to, critics insist, is rookies learning to hassle inner-city youths, to apply excessive force, and to be too quick on the trigger. The new officers also bond with the veterans to whom they are usually assigned as partners. A necessary mutual dependency is quickly established as the rookie learns that he and his partner must back each other up in situations that could become matters of life and death.

Sometimes—not often—this dependency leads the rookie into corruption. If the veteran is accepting payoffs, the rookie has three choices: participate in the graft; don't participate but say nothing; or blow the whistle on his partner. The understandable reluctance to take the third course is the basis for the "blue wall of silence," which stops otherwise honest officers from testifying against the bad apples. The "blue wall" refers to people in police uniforms sticking together and, by extension, includes all fellow officers. While the statistics show that most rookies become honest cops, many also become part of that wall of silence from the beginning of their street training.

DEALING WITH THE PROBLEMS

Many critics believe that the training steps that rookies go through are the building blocks of police corruption and brutality. However, they do not take into account the revisions in police training programs around the country that are specifically aimed at instilling resistance to brutality, corruption, and the blue wall. New courses teach conflict avoidance, verbal tactics, frequently used second languages such as Spanish, and police ethics. The New York Police Department reports that the "1996–1997 Police Academy class received more than 100 hours of anti-corruption training."[13] Also, in departments around the country, senior officers with clean records are receiving refresher courses designed to encourage them to behave as role models for new recruits.

Christine Quinn, executive director of the New York Gay and Lesbian Anti-Violence Project, and a member of the mayor's task force on police brutality, reflected the positive results of police training when she pointed out that brutal and corrupt officers "are truly, truly the minority in the Police Department. But," she added, "they are an enormous, enormous problem."[14]

It is a national problem, but new directions in training by police departments nationwide are a first big step in dealing with it. Because of such training, police spokespersons insist, the recruits who will become the officers of tomorrow will overcome the image of those few who give the police a bad name today.

CHAPTER FOUR
POLICE BRUTALITY

*"Most important of all, the police are
called into urgent situations because they,
and only they, are empowered to use
force to set matters right."*[1]

—Charles E. Silberman,
Director of the Study of Law and Justice,
a Ford Foundation Research project.

The limits of force are constantly debated both by advocates of police and their critics. The public wants officers to use whatever force is necessary to keep the peace and to protect their persons and their property from criminals. Much of the public also wants the police to use whatever force is necessary to protect their children and their neighborhoods from the plague of drugs and the violence they generate. But the public is shocked and outraged when police force is excessive and incidents of brutality and sadism are revealed. The question is: Just where is the line between necessary force and abuse of power?

ONLY HUMAN

Experienced officers will tell you that every situation is different and that the degree of force that should be used is a judgment call. Furthermore, they will point out, it is often a decision that has to be made in an instant. They do not have the leisure to ponder and weigh the fine points of their actions that those who judge them later will enjoy. The ten-year veteran of a medium-size northeastern city police force agreed to speak frankly on this matter, but didn't want his name used.

The thing is that at the time, in the actual situation, you don't have time to stop and think. And after the fact you probably can't honestly say what determined how much force you used. Did you hit the pothead with your billy because he picked up a brick? Wasn't that better than shooting him? Suppose he bashed in your skull with it? You'd be dead and then you wouldn't have to answer to Internal Affairs.

Sure, fear plays a part. She's only a crazy little old lady, but that's a butcher knife she's swinging at you. The kid you pulled over for speeding is drunk, but he puts up a fight when you cuff him and your shin's bleeding from his kick and you're only human. This is the third time you've busted this pusher a block from the schoolyard and he laughs in your face and says he'll be out of the clink before your shift is over and . . . you're only human.

Maybe you had a fight with your wife. Maybe the Captain has been riding you. Maybe you've got heartburn, or that new thing, reflux. Maybe it's just a long, hard night and opposition from a perp brings out the muscle in you. A cop can be a lamb most of the time, and just this one night the brute in him comes out. That doesn't mean he's a bad cop; it just means he's having a bad night.[2]

A GROWING NATIONAL PROBLEM

According to the National Emergency Conference on Police Brutality and Misconduct of the Center for Constitutional Rights, there was a 72 percent rise in reports of police brutality in the United States between 1992 and 1996.

Outrage at the increase peaked on October 22, 1996, with a National Day of Protest to Stop Police Brutality. Organizers reported that "thousands of people from over forty cities coast to coast, of all ages, nationalities, and classes, staged a powerful protest."[3] The point was to make people aware that police brutality wasn't only a local problem, but also a national one—and that it was spreading.

The national problem seemed to continue to grow after the 1996 demonstration. A random sampling of complaints against police in 1997 and the early part of 1998 turned up the following examples:

- Citizens Against Police Brutality protested to the St. Louis, Missouri Board of Police Commissioners that police used pepper spray (a substance which temporarily blinds and causes choking) on a mentally retarded man and beat him over the head with a nightstick after he was already subdued.

- Two Chicago officers were dismissed from the force for breaking the jaw of an eighteen-year-old while beating him with flashlights, then conspiring to cover up their actions.

• Three police officers in Naugatuck, Connecticut, were charged with "kicking, punching and stomping" on eighteen-year-old Angel Maldonado while arresting him.[4]

• An Elizabeth, New Jersey, officer who had been drinking allegedly smashed the face of a sixty-six-year-old woman, pushed her head through a window, and then attacked her seventy-year-old brother.

• In Duniway, Oregon, police strip-searched middle-school girls aged twelve to fourteen during an investigation of thefts from the school locker room.

• In Detroit the son of a local judge charged that he was beaten by the police Gang Squad while being arrested for disorderly behavior at a nightclub.

• A Conroe, Texas, police rookie charged that he witnessed two veteran officers beat up a handcuffed eighteen-year-old prisoner while two other officers stood by and watched.

AN OFFICER SPEAKS OUT

The Texas rookie was not the only one to blow the whistle on fellow officers. On January 11, 1998, NYPD officer Thomas Bennett called the Internal Affairs Bureau (the agency in police departments which investigates misbehavior by officers) to report that a prisoner being held in custody had been needlessly stripped by police, who the suspect claimed had beaten him. In April 1998, New York

City police Sergeant Gil Q. Alvarez filed a federal lawsuit charging that his superiors had ordered him to cover up evidence relating to the beating of a suspect by two detectives.

In the wake of repeated incidents of alleged police brutality in New York City, an officer who wanted to remain anonymous called Bob Herbert, a columnist for *The New York Times*. He was, the officer said, disturbed that the achievements "of many thousands of dedicated men and women in the Police Department are being undermined by officers who are arrogant, racist, sadistic, and in some cases sickeningly inhumane."[5]

He defined such officers as immature and lacking common sense. "You give them a gun and a shield and they just get power crazy. . . . They can take people's *lives*." He guessed that his criticism applied to "about 10 percent" of the officers on the force and spoke of being disillusioned by "the department's tolerance for abusive behavior."[6]

"You'll find a lot of them in narcotics," he said. He added that he had been on many narcotics raids. "They call it 'booming.' That's crashing the door down. . . . They boom the door and totally trash the apartment, but a lot of times they'll come up with nothing."[7] He described how an older women was handcuffed and dragged out into the cold during a raid in which no drugs were found.

He was asked why he didn't intervene. "You gotta work with a lotta these guys," he explained. "You go on a gun job, the next thing you know you got nobody following you up the stairs."[8]

"Booming" Victims

Botched raids in which innocent people are terrorized have taken place frequently in New York City. NYPD narcotics officers staged four of them in late February and early March

1998. On February 27, 1998, police looking for drugs mistakenly forced entry into not one but two apartments.

In the first, Ellis Elliot thought thieves were breaking into his apartment. He went to the door and called out "Who is it?"[9] When there was no answer, Elliot fired a warning shot over the top of the door. A volley of gunfire answered him. The police entered and dragged him naked into the hallway where his neighbors could see him. Then they forced him to put on women's clothes and took him to the police station. Early the next morning—some 17 hours after his arrest at 8 A.M.—police realized they had made a mistake and released him.

At 4:30 P.M. that day, while Elliot was still in jail, a dozen NYPD officers knocked down the door to Shaunsia Patterson's apartment. In the apartment with Ms. Patterson, who was eight months pregnant, were her two children, aged three and two, and her fifteen-year-old sister, Misty. The police charged in with guns drawn and seized Misty.

"They threw me face down on the floor and handcuffed me behind my back," she later told reporters. Shaunsia claims one of the officers plunged on top of her, ignoring her protests that "I'm eight months pregnant." She says that for two hours they ransacked her apartment, smashing her possessions, before they finally announced "We got the wrong apartment."[10]

A COSTLY MINORITY

Commenting on the incidents, a top NYPD official admitted that they were "bad," but nevertheless asked *New York Times* columnist Bob Herbert to "try not to smear the 38,000 people in the department" when he wrote about them.[11] Neither Herbert, nor Joseph Kelner, the lawyer representing both Shaunsia Patterson and Ellis Elliot, thought the incidents were typical of the New York City police. Kelner made a point of saying that the incidents "indicate a pattern of misconduct by a tiny minority of police officers."[12] This view is borne out by another department spokesperson who reported that "out of 45,000 drug raids conducted last year [1997], only 11 involved officers mistakenly entering a home not listed on the warrant."[13]

Actually, complaints of all kinds of police brutality seem to be falling off slightly in New York City. But this is only by comparison with a rather alarming increase over previous years. Between 1993 and 1996, "misconduct and excessive force complaints increased from 4,956 to 5,596" in the city.[14] "Judgments paid out by New York for police abuse rose from $13.5 million in 1992 to more than $24 million in 1994."[15]

In neighboring Connecticut, the state Supreme Court ruled on February 27, 1998, that citizens had the right to sue police officers personally for damages in brutality cases. The justices cited two sections of the state constitution that bar unreasonable searches and unlawful arrest. The decision was a victory for a Torrington couple, who sued the town's police chief and another officer for "entering their home without a warrant, or permission" and striking and kicking them.[16]

BACKTALK MAY PROVOKE VIOLENCE

There is a pattern in cases of police brutality. Usually it is triggered by either disrespect by, or resistance of, a suspect. One NYPD officer, bad-mouthed by a man whose dog was drinking at a public water fountain, arrested, strip-searched, and detained the man for five hours. He told the man that if people could get away with talking back, or cursing, then "tomorrow it's a stick, and the next day it's a bullet."[17]

Officers have been taught not to react to verbal abuse, but that isn't always easy to do. An article analyzing the results of challenges to police authority points out that "many officers see disrespect as a threat, not just to their job performance, but sometimes to their lives. For them, choosing to dominate testy citizens without overasserting themselves is not only an art, but an attitude."[18]

The attitude is necessary to establish authority. Insults are a challenge to that authority. The officer's adrenalin level goes up, and he or she is primed to reestablish that authority—with force if necessary.

NIGHTSTICK LESSONS

If verbal abuse is provocative, physical resistance has an even greater effect. When a suspect struggles, it is hard for an officer to call a halt to the force exercised to subdue him. Again, the adrenalin is flowing.

It also flows when a suspect runs and the officer has to chase him. She never knows if the running suspect is going to swing around and shoot at her. When she catches the suspect, exercising restraint can be a real problem.

This is particularly true in high-speed car chases. The officers' lives are at risk, and they know it. When the chase is over, their rage at having been put in danger can require a physical outlet. According to James H. Skolnick and James J. Fyfe's 1993 study of police conduct, *Above the Law*, "fleeing motorists become prime candidates for painful lessons at the end of police nightsticks."[19]

THE TARNISHED IMAGE

Unfortunately, with repetition police violence becomes easier to exercise. Some officers become hardened. Some even experience a sadistic enjoyment in resorting to violence. Ultimately, such sadism can far exceed the limits of what is appropriate.

In general the public recognizes that brutality is the exception and not the rule. Of the more than 604,000 police officers in the United States today, only a small percentage have been charged with brutality. Some of this small group have been brought up on charges again and again. This reveals a reluctance to discipline violent officers by those in charge of police departments. Nevertheless, the public generally has a good opinion of police until a shocking event shakes that opinion and an image of brutality tarnishes all officers.

THE VIOLATION OF ABNER LOUIMA

The Abner Louima case is such an incident. On August 9, 1997, Louima, a Haitian immigrant, was arrested during a brawl outside a nightclub in the New York City borough of Brooklyn. It is alleged that after being put in a patrol car, he was beaten by four officers. He was then brought to the 70th Precinct Station House where it is further alleged that he was taken into a bathroom and tortured. *The New York Times* reported that one officer is accused of holding the handcuffed Mr. Louima down while another officer "is accused of ramming a stick into Mr. Louima's rectum, inflicting severe internal injuries."[20]

Officers Justin A. Volpe, Charles Schwarz, two other officers, and a sergeant were indicted by a federal grand jury for crimes committed while depriving Mr. Louima of his civil rights. During the trial, after four fellow officers testified against him, Volpe confessed. Schwarz was found guilty, and the other three were acquitted. "Numerous rank-and-file police officers . . . [are reported to have] cooperated in the Federal investigation."[21]

Despite this cooperation, African-Americans, Latinos, and other minority groups view the Louima case as an all-too-typical example of how they risk being treated by police. It is not the white middle class that is at risk from

Protestors march outside the 70th Precinct house in Brooklyn, New York, the day after Abner Louima, who had been arrested, was violently assaulted while being held there. Not only was there a demand for justice for the alleged police brutality, but there was a call to expose the possible racial motivation for the attack.

police brutality, they say, but the poor and the downtrodden, the blacks and other minorities. Abner Louima remains a rallying point against what they perceive to be widespread police prejudice.

How widespread is this view among minorities? How justified is it? Are most officers biased? Is race really the main issue in cases of police brutality?

CHAPTER FIVE
RACE, ETHNICITY, AND GENDER

*"For the urban poor
the police are those who arrest you."*[1]
—Michael Harrington

Race was definitely the issue where police brutality was involved during the struggle for civil rights by African-Americans during the 1960s. In northern and southern cities, bigotry was often present when police dealt with protesters and tried to establish crowd control. Nonviolent demonstrations were broken up with fire hoses, police dogs, cattle prods, and the liberal use of billy clubs.

TURMOIL IN CHICAGO
Also in the 1960s, protests against the war in Vietnam were met with similar maximum-force tactics by police. During those years the line between crowd control—designed to preserve the right of the people to assemble and protest—and breaking up demonstrations blurred. The most notable example of crowd control getting out of hand was at the

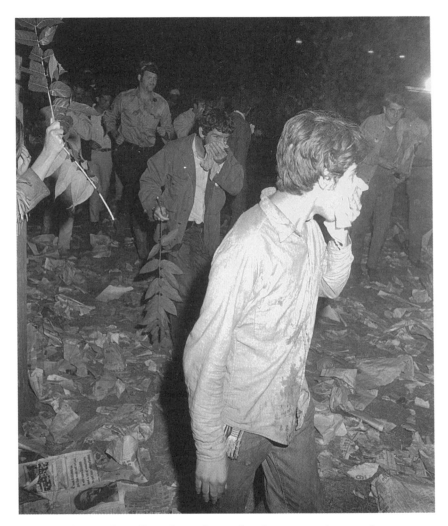

The mishandling by police of a demonstration at the 1968 Democratic National Convention in Chicago led to greater awareness of police brutality and the use of excessive force. Perhaps more fortunate than those who were beaten, these young demonstrators cover their mouths after tear gas was used to break up a crowd.

1968 Democratic National Convention in Chicago, where police who were assigned to control the crowd lost their professional cool and beat demonstrators, reporters, and innocent bystanders.

The Chicago police had just been denied a raise. There was a bus strike going on, and this, combined with the throngs of protesters who had flocked to Chicago, snarled traffic throughout the city. The officers were working double-shifts, sometimes as much as sixteen hours a day. The temperature was in the nineties. And—perhaps the final straw—some of the demonstrators called the officers "pig" to their faces and chanted the insult whenever groups of police tried to reroute the protest marchers.

Since 1968, departments around the nation have improved their handling of demonstrations and crowd control. However, when there is civil unrest, individual officers can be caught up in the action. It's not easy in the turmoil to physically control the situation without using excessive force. Many times minorities are involved, and from their point of view the officers' actions constitute police brutality. Such responses are usually not clear-cut examples of racism. But such incidents do exist.

The Rodney King Case

More than six years before the Abner Louima case in New York City, the videotaped beating of Rodney King by police officers in Los Angeles shocked the nation. Like Louima, King is a black man. He was twenty-five years old when the incident that made him famous throughout the world occurred.

It began at 12:30 A.M. on March 3, 1991, with a 7.8-mile (12.6-kilometer) highway patrol chase that reached speeds of 110 miles (177 kilometers) per hour. Finally, the speeding vehicle was pulled over at the entrance to Hansen

Dam Park. Rodney King was at the wheel, and he was drunk.

Los Angeles Police Department (LAPD) officers Lawrence Powell, Timothy Wind, Theodore Briseno, and Rolando Solano surrounded the vehicle. Sergeant Stacey Koon was in charge. He ordered Rodney King to get out of his car.

Rodney King at first ignored the command. When he did get out, he did a little dance and talked gibberish. Sergeant Koon would later testify that he thought King was on PCP, a mind-altering drug that can make the user violent and dangerous.

The officers ordered King to lie down with his hands behind his back. When he didn't comply, Sergeant Koon ordered officers Powell, Wind, Briseno and Solano to "swarm" King by jumping on his back.[2] King managed to shake the officers loose and turn on them. Sergeant Koon then shot him twice with a stun gun.

King fell to the ground, but got up again. He later said the shock from the stun gun had panicked him and he was only trying to run away. But to the sergeant, King's movements were threatening. Koon ordered Powell and Wind to subdue King with their batons.

BRUTALITY ON VIDEOTAPE

This was the point at which a man named George Holliday began videotaping the incident from the balcony of his apartment across the street. The tape shows Officer Powell swinging his baton wildly, knocking King down and continuing to strike him. A California Highway Patrol officer described seeing Powell strike the right side of King's face repeatedly. "I saw the blood come out of his face. . . . There is no doubt in my mind that he hit Mr. King repeatedly in the face."[3] The tape shows four white officers beating the

Perhaps the most widely known case of police brutality ever, the 1991 beating of Rodney King by Los Angeles police officers was captured on videotape. The violent outrage that broke out when the officers were acquitted shocked the nation and made painfully clear the racial divisions in our society.

African-American King with nightsticks, kicking him, and stomping him on the head as he lay on the ground.

Sergeant Koon, who was in command, made no effort to stop the brutality. Later he would admit: "I have seen uses of force of considerable violence, but I have not seen anything as violent as this . . ."[4] King's injuries included "a broken cheekbone and multiple fractures on the right side of his face, lacerations on the forehead, a fracture of the . . . right leg, and various bruises, contusions, and abrasions."[5]

LOS ANGELES EXPLODES

When the videotape of the beating was aired, there was international outrage. Many African-Americans saw the tape as visual evidence of police racism, which they viewed as all too common throughout the United States. In Los Angeles many members of minority groups considered the King beating a vicious example of the kind of harassment that a bigoted police force routinely inflicted on blacks, Mexican-Americans, and others.

The perception of bias grew when the April 1992 trial of Sergeant Koon and officers Powell, Wind, and Briseno for unlawful abuse of power was moved from Los Angeles to Simi Valley. Only 1.5 percent of Simi Valley residents were black, and the community was populated by thousands of police officers' families. When the trial ended with an all-white jury acquitting Sergeant Koon and Officers Wind and Briseno and unable to agree on a verdict for Officer Powell, black Los Angeles exploded in a violent riot.

It was "one of the most murderous episodes of racial violence in American history: 54 dead, 2,328 treated in hospital emergency rooms and a billion dollars of property damage."[6] For two days, black rage was directed at white people. It's important to note, however, that many blacks put their own lives in danger to protect white strangers from the mob violence.

THE AFTERMATH

The rage that was unleashed may have been triggered by the Rodney King case, but its roots went a lot deeper. According to William K. Marimow, who won two Pulitzer Prizes for his reporting on police misconduct, "the [LAPD] had a history of racism." Reviewing a book by Lou Cannon on the riots, Marimow agreed with Cannon that former Los Angeles Police Commissioner Daryl Gates's "tolerance of excessive force on the streets contributed to escalating hostility between the cop on the beat and an increasingly diverse city." A black LAPD police officer testified at a public hearing "that he worried about driving home in civilian clothes late at night because fellow officers needed no reason to stop him other than the fact that he was black."[7]

Three years after the Los Angeles riot, the National Association for the Advancement of Colored People (NAACP) and the Criminal Justice Institute at Harvard Law School issued a report titled *Beyond the Rodney King Story: An Investigation of Police Misconduct in Minority Communities*. The report found that "the weight of police abuses . . . falls disproportionately upon minority people." It cited the frequency of charges of "disorderly conduct, resisting arrest, and assault to cover [pardon] acts of [police] brutality." It found "widespread . . . police failure" in following up complaints by nonwhite citizens.[8]

Accounts of racist brutality by police around the country continued to confirm the report. In Montgomery County, Virginia, just outside Washington, D.C., the president of the local NAACP chapter charged that the county police "have engaged in a pattern and practice of racial bias."[9] A white police officer in Springfield, Massachusetts, was videotaped kicking a black suspect pinned to the ground by other officers. In Indianapolis, according to witnesses, a racial insult was shouted as sixteen white off-duty police officers who had been drinking beat up a black motorist. In New York City a black undercover officer was beaten up by a white officer during a drug bust operation.

Nevertheless, conditions have improved in Los Angeles since the riots. Officers Koon, Powell, Wind, and

Briseno were retried by a federal court on charges of depriving King of his civil rights, and in April 1993, Koon and Powell were convicted and sentenced to prison terms. Police Commissioner Gates was forced to retire. He was followed by two successive African-American police chiefs. Under their direction programs of community policing, in which officers are encouraged to establish a working relationship with the residents of the neighborhoods they patrol, has helped to change attitudes of white officers towards nonwhites and of minority civilians toward the police.

There has also been an ongoing effort by the LAPD to recruit more nonwhite officers and more women. Cross-cultural classes have been held to help all officers better understand the diverse public they serve. Such efforts are also going forward in other police departments around the country, but the role of ethnicity, gender, and race in police work is complex, and progress is slow—maddeningly slow, according to some critics of police.

MINORITY OFFICERS AT RISK

White police prejudice poses an ongoing threat to black and Latino officers in New York City, according to spokespersons for the Guardians Association, which represents 5,000 black officers, and the Latino Officers Association, which speaks for 6,000 Hispanic officers. The NYPD is 70 percent white, and most suspects are members of minority groups. For a plainclothes officer who is black or Hispanic, race-based violence—either accidental or deliberate—is a constant risk. One black undercover officer was shot by a white officer as he was confronting a woman suspect on a subway platform. When the white officer was brought up on charges, the African-American victim testified in his defense and asked for leniency for him.

THE MINORITY OFFICER

A group of minority officers—100 Blacks in Law Enforcement Who Care—charge that the NYPD itself discriminates against them. They claim that African-American and Latino officers are subjected to drug testing three times more often than white officers. They say that the testing itself is "unfair to people of color and women."[10] They cite evidence from the federal Health and Human Services Department that dark-skinned people show a higher level of drugs regardless of use and that women's hair retains more traces of opiates than men's. They also charge that "black and Latino officers are punished at higher rates than whites are."[11] The conclusion is that these factors affect test results and the statistics derived from them. It is recommended that there should be equal discipline and frequency of testing, but different standards based on skin color for African Americans and Latinos.

The problems facing minority and woman officers aren't limited to New York. Around the country, reactions to them by white policemen range from outright bigotry to subtle distancing and lack of trust. Some white officers resent being paired with a black man or a woman, and the usual bonding between police partners is either delayed or doesn't take place at all.

At the same time, the minority officer may be taunted by inner-city peers for "joining the enemy." He may be even more resented for trying to establish his authority than the white cop, from whom the attitude is expected. If he is young, he has a hard time getting respect from blacks near his own age.

MIXED ATTITUDES OF MINORITIES

Non-white civilians complain that white officers do not relate to their communities. They want more black police

*Police officers of all minority groups face special
challenges, both from the public and from other
officers. This Chinese-American officer stops to talk
with some young women on his patrol in
New York City's Chinatown.*

assigned to patrol their streets. However, nonwhite officers often feel that they are being "ghettoized" by assign-
ments to inner-city communities with high crime rates.
They know that in such neighborhoods, gang wars, drug
trafficking, and domestic violence are intensified by pov-
erty and joblessness. They share the fear of white officers
assigned to high-risk areas. All officers—black and white,
male and female—face more dangers in these areas.

The poor people who live in inner cities are the main victims of the crime and violence that the officers battle against. Effective policing is a major concern to them. Minorities around the country benefited most in 1996 when the rate for violent crime dropped 10 percent and property crime declined 8 percent. The rate continues to drop, and minorities continue to benefit. Many credit the police for these declines and are grateful to them.

At the same time, inner-city residents resent a police attitude that seems to them to be both suspicious and hostile and that too often results in minorities—particularly youth—being stopped and frisked, manhandled, and generally treated with a lack of courtesy. The attitudes of male police officers are also criticized by women's groups and gay and lesbian organizations. The complaint is that women who are arrested are not treated respectfully, nor—in cases of domestic abuse—with proper concern. Gay and lesbian suspects say they are too often treated with contempt and even sometimes physically abused by macho officers.

WHEN CULTURES CLASH

White male officers are not the only ones who act out of bias. Prejudice is a tricky thing. It can be triggered by cultural differences, gender, or sexual orientation.

An African-American police officer who has been raised in the South often does not relate any better to a black Haitian with French Caribbean traditions than a white officer who grew up in a northern suburb may to an inner-city Mexican-American. A Latino cop who is a Jehovah's Witness and a black Muslim street peddler may have little in common. A Chinese-American officer and a Korean immigrant member of a street gang do not necessarily share the same culture.

The vast ethnic mix in the United States can confuse officers. They may also have difficulties dealing with new immigrants. Language barriers (about 120 different languages are spoken in Los Angeles alone) can result in police actions escalating into violence. Many ethnic communities perceive—and resent—a lack of respect by officers of every shade for their cultures and traditions.

WOMEN OFFICERS PROVE THEMSELVES

Some of these traditions relegate women to an inferior role. In these ethnic communities, some people have problems dealing with a woman police officer who exercises her authority. Young males in particular may feel that their manhood is threatened by an aggressive female. To obey orders from a woman may label them as weak in the eyes of their peers. However, there is evidence that community policing and foot patrols have helped women officers gain respect in ethnic communities by establishing personal relations. The evidence suggests that although women officers may have further to go than male officers in overcoming ethnic suspicions, they get there just as quickly.

The first woman police officer hired in the United States was Alice Stebbins Wells, who joined the Los Angeles force in 1910. Within six years, sixteen other departments around the country had hired women. The first African-American woman officer was hired by the Buffalo, New York, Police Department in 1924.

In the beginning, there were many reservations by the public—both men and women—about women police officers. Some of those reservations still exist today. Are women physically strong enough? Are they tough enough? Can they react quickly enough? Through the centuries, police work has always been men's work. Should women really be doing it?

Despite traditional resistance to the idea of women as police, female officers have proven that they are every bit as capable at policing as their male counterparts. But like other officers in the minority, they face challenges that white male officers don't.

The record shows that women officers have proved themselves on the job. Indeed, after the adjustments of the initial break-in period, most male officers acknowledge that their women partners are competent and dependable.

Nevertheless, women are subject to some discrimination within most police departments. New York City, for instance, only just recently named its first woman precinct commander. Most departments have no women in top command positions. Women officers have to function in a basically male police culture with a tradition of regarding women as sex objects. They have to turn a deaf ear to the macho, sometimes sexual, banter of the station house. Too often they still have to prove themselves to new male partners who fear that women will lack the aggressiveness needed in life-or-death situations. Women officers may even have to deal with partners' wives who are jealous of them because of the bonds the women officers form with their husbands.

GAY OFFICERS

Probably the officers most discriminated against by other officers of all backgrounds are gays. Not so long ago it was common for police departments around the country to entrap gay citizens and arrest them for homosexual activities. The attitude that fostered that behavior is still present among some officers of every background. The very assertive attitudes that lead them to become police officers too often translate into aggressiveness and hostility toward gays—including fellow officers who are gay.

Gay and lesbian officers have to work harder to prove themselves. Like blacks and Latinos, they have organized to insist on their right to fair treatment within the various police departments across the nation. Law Enforcement Gays And Lesbians (LEGAL), with police officer members from 115 departments in 26 states, held its first annual convention in Los Angeles in 1995. Many gay officers, however, would still rather keep their sexual orientations secret than deal with institutionalized prejudice against them, or with the antigay feelings of fellow officers.

Police prejudice against gays, like racial and ethnic bigotry, is really a reflection of the bias of the society at large. But not everybody in the society is bigoted, and neither are all cops. As African-American commentator

Stanley Crouch pointed out in an article that generally praised the NYPD for "a marvelous job," while "there's no excuse for abusive treatment" by police officers, "there is also no excuse for blaming the entire department for the actions of a few."[12]

That balanced view might well be applied not just to the NYPD but to all the police departments in the country.

CHAPTER SIX
KILL OR BE KILLED

"Officers must set an example.
Guns solve nothing." [1]

—Dublin police officer;
interview April, 1992.

Police officers in many sections of Ireland, Scotland, and England do not routinely carry guns. Often they do not even carry nightsticks. While rules and regulations vary from city to city and county to county, typical restrictions on the use of firearms are those in Dundee, Scotland, where three levels of command in the police department must approve the use of guns in special situations. In an extreme emergency the highest-ranking officer on duty may issue guns. However, he or she will routinely have to justify their use—as well as any injuries that may result—to a board of inquiry.

The reasoning behind such policies is that if police don't routinely carry firearms it will lower the level of violence.

Career criminals would not be as likely to carry weapons for self-defense. People under the influence of liquor or drugs, or who are emotionally unstable, would not feel as threatened and would not react to police authority as violently. Family disputes would not escalate when officers intervene. Young people, who today commit the majority of crimes, would have greater respect for officers.

A TARGET OF OPPORTUNITY

If violence does indeed breed violence, as many believe, then reducing the firepower of police would seem a worthwhile objective. Most police officers and their commanders in the United States, however, would not agree. Crime rates in America are much higher than those of England, Scotland, and Ireland. Across America, particularly in dense population centers, officers are embattled. To disarm them, they insist, would be to reduce them to victims rather than enforcers of the law. With guns so easily available to lawbreakers, the police would be helpless without firepower to fight back.

They are often targets, they say, for no other reason than that they are police officers. Several incidents in 1997–1998 bear this out. In Long Branch, New Jersey, a 911 emergency call was made to the police from a pizza parlor. By chance, before the call could be responded to, Sergeant Patrick A. King of the Long Branch Police Department went into a Chinese take-out restaurant next door to the pizzeria. As he stood at the counter, a man came up behind him and fired two bullets from a .38 caliber revolver, killing him. An investigation concluded that the call had been intended to lure a police officer to the pizzeria to kill him. The only motive for the killing of Sergeant King was that he was a police officer.

"War with the Police"

In Denver, Colorado, a member of a skinhead hate group led police on a high-speed chase. His girlfriend drove part of the way, while he fired at pursuing officers with an automatic rifle. When he was finally cornered, he shot to death police officer Bruce Vanderjagt and then committed suicide with Vanderjagt's handgun.

A few days later a West African immigrant was shot to death at a Denver bus stop by skinheads. Later that evening, a pig's head was dumped in front of the station house where Officer Vanderjagt had served. The carcass was labeled "Vanderjagt," and a police badge was drawn under the name.[2] Subsequently, a Denver officer responding to an emergency call about a prowler was the target of a barrage of bullets from an automatic pistol.

"The pig's head said that [the skinheads] are ready to go to war with the police," noted Carl Raschke, a University of Denver professor who has studied skinheads and other white supremacist groups.[3] The bullets fired at the officer who responded to the prowler call support that conclusion.

Law-Enforcement Martyrs

All across the country, police are at risk. In Los Angeles, an officer died after being shot in the head while trying to cool down a New Year's Eve celebration that had gotten out of hand. In South Carolina a state trooper was shot and killed after pulling over a car in what should have been a routine traffic stop. In Washington, D.C., Officer Brian T. Gibson, Jr., was killed with four shots to the head at close range while sitting at the wheel of his patrol car waiting for a traffic light to change. In a precinct house in Jersey City, New Jersey, a suspect grabbed the desk lieutenant's gun and shot him twice, seriously wounding him. In Chicago, Officer James Mullen was paralyzed from the neck down by a bullet from a sniper shooting at elevated trains. In the Bronx, New York, two teenagers fired several shots at officers with a 9-millimeter Mac-11 machine pistol equipped with a laser scope.

Such incidents confirm the view of the police officers patrolling the streets that they must be prepared to protect themselves. They believe they need the best weapons available to do this. They also believe that they need the training and practice to use those weapons to their best advantage.

Weapons training for police officers continues throughout their careers. Most departments maintain pistol ranges where officers can hone their marksmanship. Fast reaction time is stressed as well as accuracy. In keeping with the philosophy of quick response and maximum force as the most effective way to deal with violent situations, the unspoken message is *Shoot to kill!*

SHOOTING TRAGEDIES

Quick-on-the-trigger reactions may save officers' lives, but civilian lives may too often be the price. Yong Xin Huang was playing with a BB gun in a friend's yard when an officer saw him and overreacted. He pulled his pistol and it misfired. The bullet struck the sixteen-year-old boy in the back of the head, killing him.

In New Haven, Connecticut, twenty-one-year-old Malik Jones was pulled over for speeding. Malik's father was a Muslim minister and a college professor. His mother was a lawyer. When Malik was stopped, he was nervous and inadvertently shifted gears into reverse. Two police officers shattered his car windows with their guns. One stuck his weapon inside the broken window where it went

The Firearms Training System (FATS)

Refresher courses in the use of firearms are a priority in big-city police departments. A recent innovation is the Firearms Training System (FATS), a computerized system described as "a little like a giant video game."[4] Officers on the firing range use laser pistols the same size and weight as the 9-millimeter semiautomatic Glocks favored by many urban police forces.

In a darkened training room, the system simulates real life. The instructor types out a scenario on a keyboard. A call garbled by static goes out over a police radio. The call may summon the officer to a robbery, a violent family quarrel, a gun battle between drug dealers, or one of a number of other situations.

Events then play out on a large screen. They require quick reactions in calling for backup, ducking for cover, shouting orders, and eventually firing guns. Instructors repeatedly tell the participants that "a split-second decision can mean the difference between living and dying."[5]

Potentially lethal gunfire is the most effective. With quick-response firing, it is easier to hit a person in the torso than in the kneecap. A body shot is also more likely to kill a person. It scores high on the laser range. It can mean death in real-life situations.

off, rapid-firing four bullets into Malik's head and killing him. The local police department, the Connecticut state attorney, and the FBI all exonerated the officer of any wrongdoing.

In Jersey City, a man with a toy gun was shot in the stomach by an officer who thought the gun was real. In Queens, New York, a seventeen-year-old high-school soccer star was shot in the leg when the candy bar he was holding was mistaken for a weapon. On St. Patrick's Day in Cleveland, when a man reached for his driver's license and pulled out his keys instead, the officer mistook the glint of metal for a weapon and fired a bullet into the suspect's buttocks. In Brooklyn, New York, a key-holder was also involved in the killing of twenty-two-year-old William J. Whitfield by Officer Michael Davitt.

TRIGGER HAPPY?

Officer Davitt was responding to a report of sniper fire from a rooftop. Whitfield was walking down the street looking for a pay phone to make arrangements with his fiancé and his children for Christmas dinner. When Davitt saw him, Whitfield seemed to be coming from the location where the shots had been fired. Davitt ordered Whitfield to stop. Whitfield, who was wanted on a minor assault and possession of marijuana charge, was afraid that if he was picked up he would have to spend Christmas in jail. He bolted.

Davitt and another officer chased Whitfield into a grocery store. Whitfield tried to hide at the back of the store. The officers shouted to him: "Drop whatever you have and step out where we can see you."[6] As Whitfield stepped out into the lights of the store, Officer Davitt fired one shot from his 9-millimeter Glock and killed him. The only thing in Whitfield's hand was "a blue knit cap that contained a large ring of keys."[7]

71 ———

Whether or not to pull the trigger is one of the toughest split-second decisions that a police officer may have to make. Therefore effective firearms training is extremely important. But does this emphasis on training make for trigger-happy cops?

Was Officer Davitt a trigger-happy cop? The question had to be asked. A grand jury cleared him of all criminal charges in the killing of William Whitfield. However, a look at Davitt's record shows that the grand jury may not have answered the question satisfactorily.

Officer Davitt had fired his weapon nine times during his fourteen-year career on the force. That was more often than any other NYPD officer. Of the 38,000 officers in the department, 93.6 percent had never fired their guns at all. Only 200 had fired their weapons more than three times in their careers. The first of the nine times Davitt used his gun was twenty-eight days after joining the force when he was assaulted at a hockey game and shot a man in the knee.

Since that time, however, Officer Davitt has made 249 arrests, "is among the top 10 percent most active officers and is highly decorated."[8] It is an impressive record. It is also an aggressive one. It raises the question of whether aggressive police work is linked to the kind of impulsive use of firearms that too often results in tragedy.

SOCIETY PAYS

The killings not only are devastating for the families of the victims, but they can also be very expensive for society. Fatalities get the largest awards in cases of police abuse. The federal civil-rights suit filed by the family of shooting victim Yong Xin Huang was settled for $400,000. In New York City alone, according to Amnesty International, awards in police brutality cases rose from $13.5 million in 1992 to $27.3 million in 1996. The bulk of this money went to the families of the victims of police killings.

In April 1998, one of the largest amounts ever for un-warranted firing by police was awarded by a jury. It was for the shooting of Darryl Barnes, which resulted not in death but in his being paralyzed from the waist down. The jury awarded him $76 million. Approving the jury's verdict, Barnes's lawyer, Robert Simels, pointed out that "people believe the police act with a great deal of excessiveness in minority areas."[9] However, the award is being appealed.

The cost to society cannot be measured only in money. In 1996 in both Leland, Mississippi, and St. Petersburg, Florida, police killed black drivers following routine traffic stops. In both cities there were riots following the shootings.

Police involved in the St. Petersburg shooting were cleared of any wrongdoing. During that same month—October, 1996—police officers who killed African-American civilians were exonerated in Pittsburgh, San Francisco, and New Brunswick, New Jersey. Friends and relatives of victims were outraged. A little more than a year later, in November 1997, a subcommittee of the House of Representatives Judiciary Committee held a hearing on killings by police in New York City.

Families of victims, "all of them black, Hispanic, or Asian,"[10] related story after story of how their relatives had been killed while the police officers responsible went unpunished. Not all of them were shot. Anthony Baez, who had asthma, died as the result of a choke hold by NYPD Officer Francis X. Livoti after Baez's football accidentally hit a squad car. Officer Livoti was acquitted of criminal charges. Subsequently, however, he was dismissed from the force.

CHOKE HOLDS AND HOG-TIED RESTRAINT

Choke holds like the one Officer Livoti used on Anthony Baez involve applying pressure to the throat from behind, usually with a nightstick, sometimes with a flashlight or an arm. The air supply is cut off. In cases of asthmatics, or people with heart disease, or suspects who have been using drugs or drinking liquor to excess, such restraint can be life-threatening. Choke holds are a frequent cause of death in arrests where firearms do not play a part.

Many departments forbid officers to use choke holds. Others lay down strict guidelines for their use. However, in cases of violent resistance, a choke hold is sometimes the only way to control a perpetrator.

Once a subject has been subdued, the problem for the officer is how to maintain the restraint. According to the FBI, most officers in such situations place perpetrators who resist "in a hog-tied and prone position by binding their hands and feet together behind their back and placing them on their stomach."[11] This position, however, "makes it difficult for subjects to breathe and can cause them to die."[12]

Some police departments refuse to authorize hog-tie tactics. However, as the FBI points out, "sometimes no other type of restraint will control a violent, aggressive subject."[13] For this reason the FBI has recommended guidelines that teach officers how to position a hog-tied subject so that he or she will breathe more easily. They explain how to monitor the subject to be sure that breathing has not become a problem.

OFF-DUTY SHOOTINGS
Some people feel that familiarity with guns and dependency on them makes it too easy for police to use them. Critics point to all-too-frequent situations in which over-zealous officers have accidentally shot bystanders and even fellow officers. They also cite deadly accidents caused by police guns in the home.

We are reminded that policing is high-stress work. The alcoholism rate among police officers is high. Sometimes officers stop off for a drink after their shift is over. Many departments require that officers carry their guns when they go off-duty. There have been instances when off-duty officers who have been drinking have settled quarrels by firing their weapons. In some instances, cops have shot marital partners and lovers with their guns. Also, there is a high rate of suicide by officers using police-issue guns.

A DELICATE BALANCE

The relationship between officers and their guns raises serious questions. Should officers who may drink alcohol be required to carry their guns when their shift is over? Should marksmanship training and refresher courses be revised to stress nonlethal targeting, rather than shooting to kill? When should an officer draw a gun? Under what circumstances should the gun be fired? Should officers have to worry about the consequences of firing their weapons when they are faced with danger? Should they be penalized for being too quick on the trigger when they may only have made the wrong split-second decision?

The answers to such questions affect officers and civilians alike. Careers and lives may depend on them. There is no bullseye to hit with these answers. But there is a need to establish a balance between necessary force and good judgment.

CHAPTER SEVEN
THE "BAD APPLES"

"In recent years the FBI has arrested police officers for corruption in every region of the nation, in large, medium-sized and small cities, towns and villages; from the inner city precincts to rural sheriff's departments."[1]

—FBI Director Louis J. Freeh,
January 21, 1998

Is there a relationship between corruption and brutality? There is no clear-cut answer. Not all violent officers are corrupt. Not all corrupt officers are violent. Yet some officers are both brutal and corrupt.

Herman Goldstein, professor of criminal justice administration at the University of Wisconsin Law School, acknowledges that police "corruption and physical abuse are sometimes inseparable." But he points out that this is not typically so. "Police have, for example, been known to use force or the threat of force to obtain payoffs. But most of the complaints alleging improper use of force do not include charges of corruption for personal gain."[2]

"Collars Make Dollars"

Personal gain is the most common element in police corruption. As one former police officer put it, "Money isn't everything, but it's what you buy everything with."[3] In other words, money is the force that makes cops go bad. That can mean a little money—or quite a lot:

- On December 14, 1995, an Atlanta police officer was convicted of stealing $500 during a drug raid.

- In early 1998 forty-four Cleveland police officers and sheriff's deputies were charged with accepting amounts up to $3,700 for providing so-called protection to a drug dealer.

- On November 25, 1997, the commander of the Washington, D.C., Metropolitan Police Department's anti-extortion unit was arrested by the FBI for allegedly extorting amounts up to $10,000 from gay men.

- On December 30, 1996, a Philadelphia police officer pleaded guilty to stealing more than $46,000 from drug dealers.

- On January 14, 1998, three Detroit police officers were charged with conspiracy to commit a robbery of roughly one million dollars.

Arrests are called *collars* in police terminology. "Collars make dollars,"[4] is the cynical motto of crooked cops. Some of them are *on the pad*, which means they are receiving regular payments for not arresting those involved in gambling, prostitution, drugs, and other illegal activities. Sometimes those on the pad take turns being *bagman*. The bagman is the one who picks up the bribes—often from organized crime contacts—every week and distributes the money among the officers, precinct commanders, and other police brass who are on the pad.

SERPICO

The vast majority of police officers in cities and towns throughout the nation are not on the pad. However, many of them know about it. Their dilemma is knowing what to do with that knowledge.

Too often, the "blue wall of silence" makes them hold their tongues. They don't blow the whistle on officers they have to work with every day. They don't risk their careers by snitching on superiors. They don't jeopardize their lives by making enemies out of those who may be guarding their backs when the bullets start to fly.

Sometimes, though, they do take such actions. The most famous officer to do so was Frank Serpico of the NYPD. From the day he joined the force in the early 1960s, Serpico made up his mind to be an honest cop. He turned down minor freebies, even a cup of coffee or a piece of fruit from merchants on his beat. He also refused to go on the pad. When he saw how high up the corruption went, he reported it to the Internal Affairs Bureau.

Serpico was transferred. That was all. No action was taken. He realized that Internal Affairs was in on the corruption. It was a pattern that continued until the Knapp Commission investigated NYPD corruption in 1971. Serpico testified before the Commission, naming names of high- and low-ranking officers. Shortly thereafter, his

*Frank Serpico was a New York City police officer
who exposed the corruption in his department
and may have paid dearly for it when later his backup
seemed to disappear during a drug raid and
Serpico was shot. Here he testifies before
the Knapp Commission in 1971.*

backup faded away during a drug raid, and Serpico was shot in the head. When he got out of the hospital, he resigned from the force. A 1973 movie starring Al Pacino celebrated his heroism.

VINNIE BLUE EYES

Another officer who testified before the Knapp Commission was David Durk. He spoke of how his pride in being a cop was "being destroyed by the corruption of the New York City Police Department, destroyed for me and for thousands of others like me." A third NYPD officer, whose reports of corruption had been overlooked and who had repeatedly been assigned to midnight-to-eight-A.M. shifts by way of punishment, was Frank Schiele. He summed up the effect of the testimony of Serpico and Durk as having "liberated rank-and-file cops from the 'shadowy deals' of their superiors."[5]

However, twenty-seven years later, in May 1998, *The New York Times* reported that anonymous undercover police Detective 4126, using the alias "Vinnie Blue Eyes," testified during the trial of an alleged drug dealer that evidence of ongoing corruption in the NYPD had been ignored by both Internal Affairs and police officials at the highest level.

His testimony was backed up by a letter on October 7, 1997, from the office of the United States attorney to the chief of Internal Affairs that accused Detective John K. Wrynn of leaking information to individuals involved in organized crime. The leaks resulted in "seriously jeopardizing the safety of two undercover detectives . . . and the confidential sources who were assisting law enforcement out on the street. In fact, we believe that both undercovers were exposed and two confidential sources were identified, one who is in fact now dead."[6]

Detective Wrynn's father was an investigator in Internal Affairs. When Detective Wrynn was first investigated in 1993, his father was "ordered not to involve himself in the investigation."[7] Despite the order, he was subsequently caught reading his son's case file. The elder Wrynn continued working in Internal Affairs for four years after the incident.

DETECTIVE 4126 IS STONEWALLED

The investigation of the Wrynns would seem to have been "scuttled by an unseen hand at Internal Affairs" from the first.[8] Orders blocking it were signed by the chief of Internal Affairs, who has since retired. In 1996, Detective 4126 wrote to NYPD Commissioner Howard Safir requesting that action be taken against the Wrynns. When asked about the commissioner's response in March, 1997, Detective 4126 replied through clenched teeth that "the Police Commissioner never got back to me."[9]

Were suspicions justified that "police brass are afraid to provoke Inspector Wrynn [by investigating him] because his position as a supervisor in Internal Affairs made him privy to potentially damaging corruption allegations about scores of police officers and commanders?"[10] Was such stonewalling done to protect the force's image or out of fear that an investigation would reveal corruption at higher and still higher levels of the police chain of command?

TOP BRASS CORRUPTION

Rank-and-file officers in most departments view their chiefs and others high up in the chain of command as political appointees and share the cynical attitudes of many citizens regarding the integrity of politicians. Is the view justified? Sometimes it is.

Chief of Police Larry Soulsby of Washington, D.C., was forced to resign in early November 1997 when a scandal broke involving a friend with whom he shared an apartment. The friend was police lieutenant Jeffery Stowe, who allegedly had been blackmailing married men who went to pickup clubs catering to homosexuals. According to an article in *The New Republic*, Chief Soulsby "personally ordered MPD [Metropolitan Police Department] auditors not to audit certain police cash accounts that Stowe controlled, and from which, law-enforcement officials say, Stowe was embezzling thousands of dollars."[11]

Former Chief of Police Alexander V. Oriente of West New York, New Jersey, and his son, a police lieutenant and supervisor of detectives, pleaded guilty on March 16, 1998, to federal racketeering and extortion charges. They had accepted bribes for protecting illegal gambling, prostitution, and after-hours liquor sales. Father and son agreed to testify against seven other members of the West New York police department who were involved in the corruption. Former Chief Oriente "admitted . . . not reporting $80,000 in bribes and kickbacks on his Federal income tax returns."[12]

The Los Angeles Times reported in December 1995 that Police Chief Willie L. Williams had accepted free rooms at a Las Vegas casino and then lied about the gift to a police commission. The commander of a New York City inner-city precinct, along with thirty-eight officers serving under him, was charged with taking payoffs and reselling confiscated firearms and drugs. In December 1996, the former Police Director of Newark, New Jersey, was sentenced to two years and six months in prison for stealing $30,000 in police funds. The Sheriff of Starr County, Texas, was charged with bribery on January 14, 1998. Three months later, high-ranking police officials in Trenton, New

Jersey, were videotaped putting quarters in slot machines and buying drinks at the bar of a social club that had not been licensed for gambling or selling alcohol.

JUDGMENT AND TEMPTATION

High-level corruption sends a message to the cops on the beat. They become aware that they are not being ordered to take action against certain criminal activities. They learn that some lawbreakers are beyond their reach, offenders with friends in high places in the department. They come to realize that certain people they arrest are to be treated with kid gloves. They watch revolving-door-justice turn loose the felons they have arrested—the drug dealers, the gambling and prostitution big shots, the organized crime kingpins—and they conclude that somebody high up is on the pad.

As Charles E. Silberman writes in *Criminal Justice, Criminal Violence*, "Even when they come in contact with respectable people, it is those people's seamier side that police often encounter. When a thief is caught with the stolen money or merchandise in his possession, police often find that the middle-class victim had exaggerated the extent of his loss in order to file a larger claim with his insurance company. Almost everywhere they turn, in fact, police encounter dishonesty and corruption, some of it petty, some of it large. Like con men, they come to believe that there is larceny in just about everyone's heart."[13]

Corruption is insidious; it can sneak up on officers. Should they accept a free cup of coffee? If they accept it every morning for a month or two, how likely are they to ticket the illegally parked car of the coffee-shop owner? Should police officers ever accept a favor or a gift from a merchant on their beat? How about a toy for the officer's child, or a roast for a family dinner? What about Christmas presents? What if the present is an envelope with a small amount of cash? What if the giver is running an illegal dice game in the back room of his store? Who does that hurt? Isn't it a victimless crime? Where should the line be drawn?

VIGORISH AND ADDICTION

The cop sees the "gift" as the so-called *vigorish* that is part of many professions. It is the cabbie short-changing a fare, the padding on the salesman's expense account, the senator's flight to Las Vegas at the taxpayers' expense. Vigorish—the small taste of corruption—is the stepping-stone to the pad.

It is also addictive. Professor Herman Goldstein writes of how an officer "comes to depend on the additional income" corruption brings. A new car, or a home, is purchased, or vacations are taken that could not have been afforded previously. The officer's standard of living rises and the result is "self-generated financial pressures." The addiction grows. "If a corrupt officer goes further and seeks to build his financial holdings through investments or gambling," he may become "predatory to the extreme." This pattern often leads from accepting gifts from lawbreakers to extorting them.[14]

A key factor fueling police corruption in today's world is illegal drugs. The traffic in marijuana, cocaine, heroin, crack, and other forbidden substances has pumped millions of dollars into the pockets of police personnel on the take. It has also weakened the morality of officers who might not otherwise succumb to temptation.

THE WAR ON DRUGS

Many officers believe that the illegal drug trade, like racial discrimination, is a nationwide problem that society has failed to solve and dumped into the laps of the police. They know that the War on Drugs has been a federal program since 1969. They believe, as do many police chiefs, that it is no closer to being won today than it was when it began.

A study of the nation's prisons by the National Center on Addiction and Substance Abuse found that "of 1.7 million prisoners in 1996, 1.4 million had violated drug or alcohol laws."[15] That adds up to 80 percent of the national prison population. All people serving sentences for crimes related to drugs were imprisoned after having first been arrested by law-enforcement officers.

Yet many officers believe that most of the drug offenders they arrest are released without serving any time at all. The higher up they are in the drug trade, the more likely felons are to walk. The most honest officers believe that this is because they buy their way out. The drug problem—along with the violence and corruption it generates—remains, and society continues to expect the cop on the beat to deal with it.

TEMPTED AND HOOKED

With so much police time being spent fighting the War on Drugs, it is inevitable that some officers will succumb to temptation. Cops' salaries are low compared with other professions. A recent survey of 322 city departments determined that the average entry level wage for a police officer was $2,152 per month.[16] When a drug bust puts an officer face-to-face with hundreds of thousands of dollars worth of cocaine or heroin, and tens of thousands of dollars in cash, the temptation to pocket a thousand or two may be too much.

Even so, most cops resist the temptation. Only a few tell themselves that taking the money of a drug dealer who will be out on the street the next day will hurt him more than the arrest does. Still fewer officers, dazzled by the dough involved, are not able to resist taking a bribe. One bribe leads to another. The greed that is generated feeds on itself and can eventually push some corrupt officers into shaking down the drug dealers for periodic payoffs.

There are also the few who can't resist sampling the drugs they seize. Some undercover police agents are forced into situations where they have to take drugs. Kim, a woman police officer, "became so hooked on cocaine that she bought it while working undercover."[17] Some police departments have programs to help drug-addicted officers.

Seizing Suspects' Assets

Another sort of corruption relating to drugs has pushed some entire police departments into distorting the law for profit. A 1984 law passed by Congress provides for an "equitable sharing" provision, which allows police to keep 80 percent of the assets seized in drug raids. These assets include cars, homes, cash, jewelry, and other property. As of 1994, "almost $1.4 billion in forfeited assets [went] to state and local law-enforcement agencies."[18]

In a suit brought against the drug task force in Oakland, California, an officer testified that police and their vehicles operated "more or less like a wolf-pack," seizing "anything and everything we saw on the street corner."[19] In Louisiana, police used money seized in drug raids for department ski trips. Similar lawlessness involving money seized under "equitable sharing" drug law enforcement has been reported in Boston, Philadelphia, Florida, and Washington State.

Most of this activity involves larger police departments. Smaller departments have neither the resources nor the opportunity to seize valuable assets from those who traffic in drugs. Drug lords don't live in small towns or rural America. They may live in the suburbs of the larger cities, and occasionally assets are seized by the larger county departments who police those suburbs, but the smaller departments are not usually involved.

THE SMALL-TOWN OFFICER

According to *Police Officer*, the preparation guide for law-enforcement employment, "over 90 percent of local police departments in the U.S. have fewer than 50 officers on their force. About half have fewer than 10 officers."[20] In the small towns and rural areas and occasional suburbs that these officers patrol, illegal drugs may be used, but they are rarely peddled. Drug buys are usually made in nearby cities with high population density. Suburban customers from Long Island, Westchester County and New Jersey, for instance, go to Washington Heights—a New York City neighborhood central to bridge and highway traffic—to buy their drugs.

Some small-town and rural officers may ignore recreational drug use in their communities as long as it doesn't lead to other criminal activity. Their situation is tricky, and corruption is more subtle. The police chief and his officers are usually hired with the approval of the local business bigwigs who run things in the town. They supply much of the tax base that supports the police department. Officers can't afford to step on their toes unnecessarily. How local laws are—or are not—enforced may reflect this.

Accommodations that can lead to petty corruption are built into this system. Parking regulations aren't enforced on sale days. Prominent citizens who drink and drive recklessly are taken home in police cars rather than arrested. If there is a labor dispute, local police discourage the picketers and may even lock them up for creating a public distur-

*A small-town police officer like this chief of police
in a Montana town may feel more directly connected to,
and held accountable by, her community than one
from a large city. This connection can be a
deterrent to corruption.*

bance. Studies have concluded that "police . . . adapt their
activities to community expectations."[21] For doing this,
their perks may include discounts at local stores, passes to
the movies, and even an occasional cash gift for overlook-
ing minor infractions of the law.

MORALITY BY EXAMPLE

Although honest small-town officers may have to tread on eggshells, they are still the majority. They may accept a slice of hot apple pie from the lady whose cat they rescued from a tree, but they don't, for the most part, take money for going along with serious criminal activity. They know that in the long run they will have to answer to all their neighbors, and they take their vow to uphold the law seriously.

In small towns and large cities throughout America many citizens believe the police have an obligation to set an example. They believe that when officers are corrupt, it undermines the most basic principles on which society depends. Police are supposed to guard the society against crime. When they become criminals, they are not just affecting their immediate victims. They are ripping off everybody. They are telling everybody—including children—that corruption is normal. That may be the worst crime of all.

Many officers resent this idea. They doubt that their profession is any more corrupt than any other profession. They point to examples of white-collar crime in every area of society. Police officers don't influence society, they say, they reflect it. And the cure for society's corruption doesn't begin with the cop on the beat. It begins with the society at large. It begins at home.

"Authority and place demonstrate and try the tempers of men by moving every passion and discovering every fraility."[1]

—Plutarch

From the earliest days of policing, there has been concern about supervision. Who will be responsible for ensuring that the actions of officers are evenhanded? Who will oversee their honesty? Who will discipline them when they violate their duty to uphold the law? *"Quis custodiet ipsos costodes?"* was the question asked by the ancient Romans—"Who guards the guardians?"[2]

DISCIPLINE VS. FRIENDSHIP: A SMALL-TOWN DILEMMA

In small U. S. police departments, it is the chain of command that oversees officers. Infractions of rules are handled in an up-the-ladder manner with officers responsible to sergeants, sergeants to lieutenants, deputies to sheriffs, and so on. Serious cases of brutality and corruption are usually judged by the small-town chief of police, or the local sheriff. That person will have the authority to decide if an officer or deputy is guilty, or not guilty; and whether to keep the offender on the force, let him or her off with a reprimand, discharge the officer, or press criminal charges. In some cases the chief or sheriff will act in concert with a police advisory board, or even a political group such as the town's selectmen.

Local politics may affect decisions in the handling of cases of police corruption and brutality. The corruption of an officer may involve the higher-ups who hold his or her fate in their hands. The officer in an all-white rural community who beats up a nonwhite out-of-town speeder may actually be reflecting the prejudices of those who do the hiring and firing on the force. The *status quo* may outweigh justice when people of influence in a small community pass judgment on their police.

The chief of police or local sheriff is caught in the middle. In small towns and rural communities, the class distinctions between the chief of police, or local sheriff and the deputies or beat officers on, for instance, a force of twenty are not likely to be very great. They may go to the same church, belong to the same lodge, even have the same relatives. Justice may sometimes be tempered with more mercy than the police offender legitimately deserves. How can the chief comfortably fire the son of the local merchant he plays poker with every Friday night?

The problems of supervising police in small towns and rural areas are all-too human problems. Not just self-interest, but personal relationships that may be complicated and long-term are involved. It's hard to do the right thing when it may seriously affect officers you've known all their lives and will probably go on knowing after you've disciplined them. Conscience is a tricky matter when small-town friendships are involved.

INTERNAL AFFAIRS: OUT OF THE LOOP

In cities, decisions concerning the criminality of police officers are usually handled by a bureau or division of Internal Affairs. These are units within police departments charged with investigating, apprehending, and sometimes disciplining officers involved in activities that violate department rules. These may involve brutality, corruption, or less serious matters such as leaving cars in illegal parking zones, *cooping* (grabbing a quick nap while on duty), sloppiness of uniform dress, careless handling of weapons, filling out reports incorrectly, exaggerating arrest figures, using foul language, and others.

The scope of responsibilities of Internal Affairs can work against its effectiveness. Police officers who feel that they themselves are being policed and at risk for punishment for minor infractions of rules tend to resent Internal Affairs as a disciplinary body out to get them. The loyalty that officers develop toward one another often excludes Internal Affairs officials. An "us" versus "them" mind-set develops.

This discourages honest cops from becoming whistle-blowers. If your partner doesn't turn you in for cooping, you're not apt to turn him or her in for whacking a perp too hard with a nightstick. If your buddy overlooks you blowing your cool with a dope peddler, you're not going to rat on him or her for pocketing a nickel bag of pot. It builds from there, and for most cops, including the majority who are honest and don't use excessive force, Internal Affairs is simply out of the loop.

THE FOX GUARDING THE HENHOUSE

The procedures that Internal Affairs sets up discourage honest cops from going to them, says David Durk, a former NYPD detective who fought corruption within the department. Durk describes a 1986 effort to involve Internal Affairs in the case of Michael Dowd, a rogue officer whose testimony six years later would blow open a police corruption scandal of major proportions. Internal Affairs, according to Durk, "wouldn't do anything unless the cop [who was trying to blow the whistle on Dowd] agreed to come forward, identify himself, and wear a wire." Durk points out the position in which such a demand places an honest cop. "Either you stand up and say, *'J'accuse,'* and your career is over, or you go away."[3] The choices reflect how strongly the majority of officers have traditionally felt about a snitch in blue who betrays one of their own. That attitude has been changing, however.

Another thing that works against Internal Affairs departments in many cities is the pressure to protect the police department's image. The way this works is that Internal Affairs may put a lot of effort into nabbing and prosecuting individual officers, but they stay away from the kind of investigation that might reveal system-wide corruption. Both the reputation of the department and concern about identifying higher-ups who can influence their careers contribute to this kind of caution.

Finally, there is the corruptibility of Internal Affairs investigators themselves. Most of them, like most officers in general, are honest and try to do the best job they can. But a certain percentage, as with all officers, are corrupt. The difference is that their position in Internal Affairs gives them the power to conceal corruption in the department, to get rid of evidence, and sometimes even to frame those honest officers who are trying to clean things up. A corrupt officer in Internal Affairs is, in effect, like a fox guarding the henhouse.

COMPLAINT REVIEW BOARDS

In some cities charges against officers made by Internal Affairs or through other channels are followed up by complaint review boards. Some of these review boards are composed of police officers. Some are made up of civilians appointed in consultation with police officials and members of police societies. Some are made up of civilians appointed by mayors, heads of counties, borough presidents, and/or other government officials. A very few are independently chosen by bodies not connected with either the police department or the city government.

Police advocates insist that only police can understand the pressures of the job well enough to fairly judge fellow officers. Critics protest that only a civilian complaint review board free of pressure from the department can be effective. Sometimes there are attempts at compromise.

THE NEW YORK REVIEW BOARD BATTLE

In New York City a thirteen-member Civilian Complaint Review Board was appointed by the mayor (who named five board members including the chairman), the City Council (which appointed one board member from each of the city's five boroughs), and the police commissioner (who selected three with law-enforcement experience). This compromise did not satisfy those who wanted an independent civilian complaint review board.

Representatives of minority groups in particular were outraged. As time passed their outrage grew, and with good reason. *The New York Times* reported that the Board received "20,000 misconduct allegations . . . in its four years of existence [and] only one officer has been dismissed."[4]

As of 1998, the board had a large backlog of cases due to understaffing and underfunding.

Twice, the New York City Council voted to create a Civilian Complaint Review Board independent of the NYPD and political pressures, a board that would be adequately funded. Twice Mayor Rudolph Giuliani vetoed the bill. In autumn 1997, the council voted overwhelmingly to override the veto. On March 26, 1998, the mayor sued to block creation of the new board. "The Mayor," said City Council President Peter Vallone, "[believes] that corruption within a police department can best be handled by the police department. We think that history has conclusively determined otherwise."[5] That is the argument, in a nutshell.

THE PHILADELPHIA PROGRAM

In other cities grass-roots efforts have been mounted to create independent review authorities. In San Francisco the Bay Area Police Watch Project is gaining support. So too are efforts in Los Angeles, Phoenix, and Pittsburgh. In Connecticut, however, the state legislature killed a measure to establish an independent board because of opposition by the police union.

The most far-reaching effort was launched in Philadelphia in September 1996. "An agreement to combat police corruption" settled a suit by the NAACP and its Philadelphia branch and the Police Barrio Relations Project against the City of Philadelphia.[6] It established a fifteen-member "Independent Commission to Study Police Corruption and Misconduct."[7] It allowed lawyers from the NAACP, the American Civil Liberties Union (ACLU), and the Police Barrio Relations Project to monitor "efforts to systematically weed out corruption from its [Philadelphia's] 6,000-member police force."[8] One of the twenty-one re-

*Most agree that a key factor in maintaining
police integrity is the policing of the force itself.
Keeping a balance, however, of what is fair to both the
police and ordinary citizens is no small task. As
evidenced by this 1990 New York City demonstration,
the two sides can be blatantly at odds.*

forms spelled out in the agreement was "a reporting system in which officers would bypass the normal channels and report police misconduct through a separate chain of command."[9]

Although the agreement had been the outcome of scandals involving brutality, robberies by officers, and the framing of suspects, the local police union opposed it. They insisted "that the reforms will hamper the ability of the officers to do their job on the street."[10] But within five months of the signing of the agreement, the city paid out more than $3.5 million to settle lawsuits brought against the police.

POLICE VS. FBI

The agreement allowed the FBI to probe corruption in the Philadelphia Police Department. As a result, eleven officers were brought up on charges. Some 150 cases based on the officers' arrests and testimony were thrown out.

Predictably, the FBI probe angered the Philadelphia police union. Their anger was not as great, however, as that of members of the Fraternal Order of Police in Prince Georges County, which borders Washington, D.C. Investigations by the FBI of abuse complaints involving minority citizens, including the beating of a handcuffed suspect, provoked an editorial in the order's newsletter that "urges officers to stop cooperating with the FBI." The newsletter's cover proclaimed in large, bold letters: "The FBI are the warriors who come on to the battlefield after the battle and bayonet the wounded."[11]

Probes by the FBI and others into police department misbehavior are always resented. Too often there is no cooperation during the investigation and no action after it is over. In 1992 the Los Angeles Christopher Commission investigated the police department and identified dozens of officers who were corrupt or had behaved brutally. None of the officers were fired. Some of them have since been involved in new instances of brutality or corruption.

THE KNAPP COMMISSION

There have been many local police investigative agencies like the Christopher Commission. Two of the most famous probed corruption in the NYPD. The first, which functioned from 1970 through 1972 was the Knapp Commission, named for its chairman, Whitman Knapp, a former New York City prosecutor.

The Knapp Commission uncovered police bribery involving organized crime. Cops on the pad were allowing narcotics trafficking and prostitution to flourish in New York City. According to the *Encyclopedia of Crime*, "bribes to police added a full five percent to construction costs" in the city. The commission determined that "police officers took at least $4 million in bribes annually." The Police commissioner, however, objected that "the Commission had gone too far and was ruining the reputation of honest officers."[12]

The commission's final report asked: "Will history repeat itself? Or does society finally realize that police corruption is a problem that must be dealt with and not just talked about once every twenty years?" A decade later "knowledgeable newsmen more or less agreed that while corruption and graft still existed, abuses definitely had not reached pre–Knapp Commission levels."[13]

In September 1992 the Mollen Commission, headed by Judge Milton Mollen, a former New York City deputy mayor, cast doubt on that conclusion. Their investigation uncovered officers working in teams to either protect, shake down, or rob drug dealers. Some of the officers dealt drugs themselves. Michael Dowd, who cut a deal to testify before the commission, described how he and other officers would meet on the shore of a Jamaica Bay inlet to "drink, laugh, fire off their guns and plan their freelance drug raids."[14] The investigation eventually tarnished whole precincts and their commanders.

JUSTIFYING GRAFT

New York City may draw the most national attention, but it is far from the worst example of police criminality in the United States. As long ago as 1950, the Kefauver Anti-Crime Committee, headed by Senator Estes Kefauver of Tennessee, uncovered a pattern of graft and payoffs by criminals to law-enforcement officials in many locales across the nation.

In Chicago, Captain Dan Gilbert, reputed to be "the world's richest cop," admitted that his command had not raided a bookie joint in twelve years. In Louisiana, sheriffs and marshals "somehow had gotten very rich" by not closing illegal gambling casinos run by organized crime. In New Orleans the chief of detectives, who earned $186 a month, "managed to squirrel away some $150,000 in a safe-deposit box."[15]

Twenty years later the Police Foundation surveyed police corruption throughout the country. They determined that "30 states reported allegations of corruption at all levels, in small-town, suburban, big city, county, and state police forces." The attitude among officers then was that "police graft is a trifling part of a pattern that includes much greater graft taking by public officials."[16]

INTEGRITY IS WINNING

Many people think that police are as corrupt and brutal today as in 1950, or in the 1970s, if not more so. They look at the 1992 Mollen Commission report and see little improvement in the NYPD. The newspapers report that Miami officers stole 1,000 pounds (454 kilograms) of cocaine and resold it, that four police officers in New Orleans are charged with murder, and that forty officers in Cicero, Illinois, have been suspended for "misdeeds that include extortion."[17] Every day seems to bring new police scandals in other towns and cities.

Have all the special commissions and probes and investigations been in vain? Actually, no. Historically, the publicity generated by commissions, probes, and even police scandals, raises public awareness. When that happens, cases of corruption and brutality decrease.

Every time an honest cop testifies before a commission, that sends a message to the majority of other honest cops that silence in the face of corruption and brutality is not part of their job description. Change may come slowly, but the evidence is that in police departments around the country the "blue wall of silence" is crumbling.

AFTERWORD

"A policeman's lot is not a happy one . . ."[1]
— "Pirates of Penzance,"
Act Two, by W. S. Gilbert

One thing that becomes clear from studies of police misconduct is the influence of those in charge on the conduct of rank-and-file officers. When brutality charges are winked at by superiors, the violence escalates. When so-called wrongful deaths by trigger-happy officers are defended by the establishment, a dangerous standard is established. Bigotry at the top encourages racism in the ranks. Corruption in high places in police departments breeds corruption all the way down the organizational ladder to the cop on the beat. Treating whistle-blowers as troublemakers reinforces the code of silence that protects police criminality.

TOP-DOWN REFORM
Today the responsibility of top police brass is being reassessed. Once department reforms began with shake-ups

from the ground up. Today it is the person at the top of a troubled department who is being scrutinized. The result is that police chiefs and commissioners are being replaced with an eye toward establishing new standards of sensitivity, attitude, and behavior.

Top police officers are being sought to head troubled departments, and top salaries are being offered them. This has led to bidding wars in problem cities like Philadelphia, Chicago, New Orleans, Los Angeles, San Jose, California and others. Chiefs and commissioners who have demonstrated that they know how to keep violence and corruption at a minimum are the most sought after. "It's a much different emphasis from years ago" according to Dan Rosenblatt, executive director of the International Association of Police Chiefs.[2]

In the lower ranks, for the most part, the quest for the best commanders is welcomed. Officers of all races and ethnic backgrounds, both male and female, want to look up to the person in charge. They want someone to set standards they can respect. They want those standards to be enforced.

THE HARD CHOICES

Those standards are the rules that officers are supposed to live by. However, it's not always easy to do that. What makes sense as department policy is not always so clear-cut on the beat. Things happen quickly, snap judgments must be made, and knowing what to do can be a difficult task.

Nevertheless, a police officer must make the hard choices. These choices don't have to be made every day, perhaps, but they must be faced often enough to be considered a fundamental part of the job. For example:

• An officer witnesses a late-night purse snatching, and she chases the perpetrator into a dark alley. As she runs into the alley, the suspect wheels around to face her. The moonlight catches the glint of a shiny object in his hand. Should the officer fire? If she doesn't, she could be killed herself. If she fires and the perpetrator is killed and the glint turns out to be from his keys or some other object, she could be brought up on charges.

• An officer tries to arrest a disorderly addict high on drugs, and the addict becomes violent. The officer is in danger of being hurt—perhaps badly. If the officer uses a choke hold—a life-threatening tactic for the suspect when drugs are involved—he will be breaking regulations handed down from the U.S. Department of Justice. But if he backs off from the situation, he is turning loose a potential menace to society.

• Perhaps an officer hears cries of "Stop, thief!" from around a corner. She sees two men—one white, one black—walking briskly down the deserted street, away from the sound of the shouts. They are on opposite sidewalks. She can't stop them both. If she stops the white man and the black man is the perpetrator, he will get away. If she decides to stop the black man, she may have made a racist decision. If he is innocent, she may have to account for her racism, perhaps even face charges. But if she stops neither man, the perpetrator will not be caught.

• An undercover officer working on a major corruption scandal aimed at prosecuting an organized crime kingpin must pretend to be corrupt. An underling of the gang lord offers the officer a stolen set of expensive electric trains for his son. If the officer turns the gift down, he will blow his cover. But if he accepts the trains, he will be participating in the corruption he is investigating and his credibility will be open to question.

• A rookie sees the partner who is teaching her the ropes accept a white envelope from a known drug dealer. If she reports the incident to Internal Affairs, she will be labeled a snitch just as her career is beginning. If she doesn't, she knows she will be starting off her career on the wrong foot.

THE ULTIMATE RESPONSIBILITY

We all have to make decisions. Few of us, however, have to make them as often, or as quickly, or as rife with serious consequences that are open to error as police officers do. In some ways, it is easy to forgive them their mistakes.

That is not to say, though, that police officers should not be held accountable for their decisions. Police brutality, corruption, bigotry, and trigger-happy responses are serious and ongoing problems. Despite understanding the difficulties that officers face, procedures must be established to help them deal with these problems. In the end, the answer to the question "who guards the guardians" is that it is the responsibility of us all.

SOURCE NOTES

CHAPTER ONE

1. Carl Sifakis, *The Encyclopedia of American Crime* (New York: Facts on File, 1982), p. 736.

2. Eric H. Monkhonen, "The Mystery of Crime's Decline," *St. Petersburg Times*, December 28, 1997, p. 1D.

3. Ibid.

4. Author uncredited, "Killing of Police Officers Rose in '97, F.B.I. Says," in *The New York Times*, May 12, 1998, p. A1.

5. Author uncredited, *Police Officer: The Complete Preparation Guide* (New York: Learning Express, 1996), Chapter 1, p.16.

6. Ibid.

CHAPTER TWO

1. Carl Sifakis, *The Encyclopedia of American Crime* (New York: Facts on File, 1982), p. 578.

2. Ted Gottfried, *The American Media* (New York: Franklin Watts, 1997), p. 35.

3. Carl Sifakis, *The Encyclopedia of American Crime* (New York: Facts on File, 1982), p. 448.

4. Ibid.

5. Ted Gottfried, *The American Media* (New York: Franklin Watts, 1997), p. 35.

6. Carl Sifakis, *The Encyclopedia of American Crime* (New York: Facts on File, 1982), p. 578.

7. Rick Bear and Leslie Cohen Berlowitz, eds., *Greenwich Village: Culture and Counterculture* (New Brunswick: Rutgers University Press, 1993), p. 130.

8. Carl Sifakis, *The Encyclopedia of American Crime* (New York: Facts on File, 1982), pp. 704–705.

CHAPTER THREE

1. David Kocieniewski and Kevin Flynn, "New York Police Lag in Fighting Domestic Violence by Officers," *The New York Times*, November 1, 1998, p. 40.

2. *Courtesy. Professionalism. Respect.* (Published by Police Department, City of New York, August 1997), p. 5.

3. Ibid.

4. Duayne Draffen, "55 Suffolk County Officers Accused of Lying on Hiring Exams," *The New York Times*, February 27, 1998, p. B5.

5. Ibid.

6. David Kocieniewski, "Mayor Backs Raising Pay For Beat Patrol," *The New York Times*, March 26, 1998, p. B7.

7. David Kocieniewski, "Plan Is Seen for New Class of Officers," *The New York Times*, March 24, 1998, p. B1.

8. Jeffrey Rosen, "Damage Control," *The New Yorker*, February 23 and March 2, 1998, p. 68.

9. Jan Hoffman, "Police Tactics Chipping Away at Suspects Rights," *The New York Times*, March 29, 1998, p. 40.

10. Ibid.

11. Author uncredited, *Police Officer: The Complete Preparation Guide* (New York: Learning Express, 1996), Chapter 1, p. 3.

12. Author Uncredited, "Police Violence," *Black Scholar*, Spring 1997, p. 60.

13. *Courtesy. Professionalism. Respect.* (Published by Police Department, City of New York, August 1997), p. 10.

14. Dan Barry, "Giuliani Dismisses Police Proposals by His Task Force," *The New York Times*, March 27, 1998, p. B5.

CHAPTER FOUR

1. Charles E. Silberman, *Criminal Violence, Criminal Justice* (New York: Random House, 1978), p. 204.

2. Author's Interview, New Haven, Connecticut, April 13, 1998.

3. Author uncredited, "Police Violence," *Black Scholar*, Spring 1997, p. 59.

4. "Teen Files Lawsuit Against Police," *The Connecticut Post*, March 1, 1998, p. A11.

5. Bob Herbert, "A Cop's View," *The New York Times Week in Review*, March 15, 1998, p. 17.

6. Ibid.

7. Ibid.

8. Ibid.

9. Bob Herbert, "Day of Humiliation," *The New York Times Week in Review*, March 8, 1998, p. 17.

10. Bob Herbert, "Reprise of Terror," *The New York Times*, June 9, 1997, p. 22; March 12, 1998, p. A27.

11. Ibid.

12. Ibid.

13. Kit R. Roane, "Once Again, Police Raid the Wrong Apartment," *The New York Times*, March 21, 1998, p. B1.

14. *Tough Cops, Thin Skin*, Editorial in *The New York Times*, November 22, 1997, p. A14.

15. Author uncredited, "When Justice Kills," *The Nation*, June 9, 1997, pp. 21-23.

16. Author uncredited, "Suits in Cop Searches Upheld," *The Connecticut Post*, March 1, 1998, p. A5.

17. Deborah Sontag and Dan Barry, "Disrespect as Catalyst for Brutality," *The New York Times*, November 19, 1997, p. B6.

18. Ibid., p. A1.

19. Author uncredited, *Time*, November 19, 1997, p. B6.

20. Joseph P. Fried, "Prosecutors Building a Case for a Federal Louima Trial," *The New York Times*, February 20, 1998, p. B4.

21. Joseph P. Fried, "U.S. Takes Over Prosecution of Police Officers in Attack," *The New York Times*, February 27, 1998, p. B5.

CHAPTER FIVE

1. John Bartlett, *Bartlett's Familiar Quotations*, Fourteenth Edition (Boston: Little, Brown and Company, 1968), p. 1082A.

2. Lou Cannon, "The King Beating: More Than Met the Eye on Videotape," *The Washington Post*, January 25, 1998, p. A10.

3. Ibid.

4. Ibid., p. A1.

5. Ibid., p. A11.

6. Christopher Caldwell, "Anatomy of a Riot," *The Wall Street Journal*, February 5, 1998, p. A19.

7. William K. Marimow, "Doing the Wrong Thing," *The New York Times Book Review*, February 8, 1998, p. 21.

8. Paul G. Chevigny, "Beyond the Rodney King Story," *Contemporary Sociology*, November 1996, pp. 798–799.

9. Manuel Perez-Rivas, "Lawmaker Proposes Police 'Mediator,'" *The Washington Post*, March 17, 1998, p. B8.

10. Alice McQuillan, "Black Cops' Group Charges Bias," *The New York Daily News*, February 23, 1998, p. 22.

11. Ibid.

12. Stanley Crouch, "Wanted in '98: One Standard for Cop Conduct," *The New York Daily News*, January 1, 1998, p. 33.

CHAPTER SIX

1. Ted Gottfried, *Gun Control* (Brookfield, Connecticut: The Millbrook Press, 1993), p. 76.

2. James Brooke, "Spate of Skinhead Violence Catches Denver by Surprise," *The New York Times*, November 21, 1997, p. A18.

3. Ibid.

4. Michael Cooper, "Zapping the Way to Better Police Marksmanship," *The New York Times*, March 7, 1998, p. B6.

5. Ibid.

6. Robert D. McFadden, "After Man Is Slain by Officer, Anger and Calls for Patience," *The New York Times*, January 27, 1997, p. B1.

7. Ibid.

8. Alice McQuillan, "Cops Who've Shot Facing City Review," *The New York Daily News*, January 1, 1998, p. 8.

9. David Rohde, "$76 Million for Man Shot by the Police," *The New York Times*, April 9, 1998, p. B6.

10. Ellis Henican, "Meet the New Rudy, Same as the Old Rudy," *Newsday*, November 19, 1997, p. A5.

11. *FBI Law Enforcement Bulletin*, May 1996, p. 22.

12. Ibid.

13. Ibid., p. 24.

CHAPTER SEVEN

1. Press Release, FBI National Press Office, January 21, 1998, p. 1.

2. Herman Goldstein, *Policing a Free Society* (Cambridge, Massachusetts: Ballinger Publishing Company, 1977), p. 188.

3. Author's interview with retired Minneapolis police officer, Guadeloupe, French West Indies, December 10, 1997.

4. Herman Goldstein, *Policing a Free Society* (Cambridge, Massachusetts: Ballinger Publishing Company, 1977), p. 194.

5. James Lardner, *Crusader* (New York: Random House, 1996), p. 213.

6. David Kocieniewski, "The Test of a Detective's Loyalty:

Stepping Over the Thin Blue Line," *The New York Times*, May 4, 1998, p. B4.

7. Ibid.

8. Ibid.

9. Ibid.

10. Ibid.

11. Carl T. Rowan Jr., "D.C. Confidential," *The New Republic*, January 19, 1998, p. 20.

12. David M. Herszenhorn, "Ex-Police Chief and His Son Plead Guilty in Corruption," *The New York Times*, March 17, 1998, p. B5.

13. Charles E. Silberman, *Criminal Violence, Criminal Justice* (New York: Random House, 1978), p. 239.

14. Herman Goldstein, *Policing a Free Society* (Cambridge, Massachusetts: Ballinger Publishing Company, 1977), p. 200.

15. Christopher S. Wren, "Drug or Alcohol Linked to 80% of Inmates," *The New York Times*, January 9, 1998, p. A14.

16. Author uncredited, *Police Officer: The Complete Preparation Guide* (New York: Learning Express, 1996), Chapter 1, p. 5.

17. Christopher S. Wren, "The Disease That Does Not Discriminate," *The New York Times Television* magazine, January 29, 1998, p. 4.

18. Eric Blumenson & Eva Nilsen, "The Drug War's Hidden Economic Agenda," *The Nation*, March 9, 1998, p. 12.

19. Ibid., p. 15.

20. Author uncredited, *Police Officer: The Complete Preparation Guide* (New York: Learning Express, 1996), Chapter 1, p. 9.

21. *Encyclopaedia Britannica*, Volume 14 (Chicago: Encyclopaedia Britannica Inc., 1984) p. 667.

CHAPTER EIGHT

1. John Bartlett, *Bartlett's Familiar Quotations*, Fourteenth Edition, (Boston: Little, Brown and Company, 1968), p. 136B.

2. *Encyclopaedia Britannica*, Volume 14 (Chicago: Encyclopaedia Britannica Inc., 1984), p. 662.

3. James Lardner, *Crusader* (New York: Random House, 1996), p. 339.

4. Michael Cooper, "New York Undercounted Civilian Complaints About Police," *The New York Times*, December 11, 1997, p. B12.

5. Norimitsu Onishi, "Giuliani Sues to Block Police Board," *The New York Times*, March 26, 1998, p. B7.

6. *Civil action No. 96-6045, Federal Court,* J. Stewart Dalzell presiding, p. 1.

7. Ibid.

8. Roberto Rodriguez and Patricia Gonzales, "Philadelphia Tackles Police Corruption," *Chronicle Features*, September 27, 1996, p. 1.

9. Ibid.

10. Ibid.

11. Philip P. Pan, "Police Union Assails FBI," *The Washington Post*, April 23, 1998, p. D1.

12. Carl Sifakis, *The Encyclopedia of American Crime* (New York: Facts on File, 1982), p. 402.

13. Ibid.

14. James Lardner, *Crusader* (New York: Random House, 1996), p. 335.

15. Carl Sifakis, *The Encyclopedia of American Crime* (New York: Facts on File, 1982), p. 388.

16. Ibid., p. 628.

17. Dirk Johnson, "Cicero Journal," *The New York Times*, May 12, 1998, p. A11.

AFTERWORD

1. John Bartlett, *Bartlett's Familiar Quotations*, Fourteenth Edition (Boston: Little, Brown and Company, 1968), p.766B.

2. Michael Janofsky, "Flush and Crime-Wary Cities Bid Up Pay for Police Chiefs," *The New York Times*, April 10, 1998, p. A12.

ORGANIZATIONS TO CONTACT

Afro-American Police League
PO Box 49122
Chicago, IL 60649
Phone: (773) 568-7329

American Civil Liberties Union (ACLU)
132 W. 43rd Street
New York, NY 10001
Phone (212) 944-9800

American Federation of Police and Concerned Citizens
3901 Biscayne Boulevard
Miami, FL 33137
Phone: (305) 573-0070

American Police Academy
1000 Connecticut Avenue N.W., Suite 9
Washington, D.C. 20036
Phone: (202) 293-9088

Amnesty International Of the U. S. A.
322 8th Avenue
New York, NY 10001
Phone: (212) 807-8400

International Association of Chiefs of Police (IACP)
515 North Washington Street
Alexandria, VA 22314
Phone: (703) 836-6767

Law Enforcement Gays and Lesbians (LEGAL) International
P.O. Box 1161, Old Chelsea Station
New York, NY 10011-1161

National Association of Police Organizations (NAPO)
750 1st Street N.W., Suite 920
Washington, D.C. 20002-4242
Phone: (202) 842-4420

National Black Police Association (NBPA)
3521 Mount Pleasant Street N.W.
Washington, D.C. 20010-2103
Phone: (202) 986-2070.

INTERNET SITES

(All have links to related sites)

American Civil Liberties Union (ACLU)—www.aclu.org

Cecil Greek's Criminal Justice Page (created by a professor of Criminal Justice at the University of Southern Florida)—www.stpt.usf.edo/~greek/cj.html

Cop Net & Police Resource List—police.sas.ab.ca

Government Accountability Project (reports on whistle blowers)—www.halcyon.com/tomcgap

Human Rights Watch—www.hrw.org

Law Enforcement Sites on the Web—www.geopages.com/CapitolHill/1814/ira.html

NAACP Online—www.naacp.org

National Urban League—www.nul.org

Office of International Criminal Justice—www.acsp.uic.edu/index.html

Police Officers' Internet Directory—www.officer.com

U.S. Federal Government Agencies—www.lib.lsu.edu/gov/fedgov.html

FURTHER READING

Anderson, Kelly C. *Police Brutality*. San Diego: Lucent Books, 1995.

Author uncredited. *Police Officer: The Complete Preparation Guide.* New York Learning Express, 1996.

Bornstein, Jerry. *Police Brutality: A National Debate.* Hillside, NJ: Enslow Publishers, 1993.

Cannon, Lou. *Official Negligence: How Rodney King and the Riots Changed Los Angeles and the LAPD.* New York: Times Books, 1987.

Gates, Daryl F., with Diane K. Shah. *Chief: My Life in the LAPD.* New York: Bantam Books, 1993.

Goldstein, Herman. *Policing a Free Society.* Cambridge, Massachusetts: Ballinger Publishing Company, 1977.

Miller, Maryann. *Everything You Need to Know About Dealing With the Police.* New York: Rosen Group, 1995.

Owens, Tom, with Rod Browning. *Lying Eyes: The Truth Behind the Corruption and Brutality of the LAPD and the Beating of Rodney King.* Emeryville, CA: Thunder's Mouth Press, 1994.

Sifakis, Carl. *The Encyclopedia of American Crime.* New York: Facts on File, 1982.

Silberman, Charles E. *Criminal Violence, Criminal Justice.* New York: Random House, 1978.

Wirths, Claudine G. *Choosing a Career in Law Enforcement.* New York: Rosen Group, 1996.

GLOSSARY

bagman—the officer who collects payoffs and distributes them to other officers.

baton—a club used to subdue lawbreakers; also known as a nightstick or billy club.

beat—the area an officer patrols.

billy club—another name for a baton or nightstick. See *baton*.

blue wall of silence—the tacit understanding among officers that they will not turn in one another for wrongdoing.

booming—breaking down a door with maximum force to raid an apartment.

civilian complaint review board—a body independent of a police department that deals with complaints against officers.

collar—police slang for arrest.

community policing—officers working with the residents of an area to control crime.

complaint review board—a body dealing with officer misconduct and usually having some connection to a police department.

constable—a peacekeeper in colonial America.

cooping—taking a nap or goofing off while on duty.

drug bust—police action to arrest narcotics dealers.

"Equitable Sharing"—a section of a 1984 federal law that allows police to keep 80 percent of the assets seized in drug raids.

excessive force—use of physical police power beyond what is needed to restrain a suspect.

firearms training seminar (*FATS*)—a computerized firearms training system like a giant video game.

Glock—the 9-millimeter, semiautomatic pistol favored by many police departments.

gun job—a raid by police using firearms.

internal affairs—the bureau within a police department which monitors officer misbehavior.

jackroller—mugger.

leatherheads—colonial constables who wore heavy leather helmets.

maximum force policy—the police tactic of striking quickly and hard in order to defuse a situation before it can gather momentum.

Miranda rights—a suspect's right to remain silent and to have a lawyer present during questioning.

nightstick—another name for a baton or billy club. See *baton*.

night watch—colonial constables who patrolled between dusk and dawn.

on the pad—an officer taking kickbacks or accepting bribes on a regular basis.

pad—a group of officers who work together illegally for profit.

perp—the perpetrator of a crime.

pothead—addicted user of marijuana.

quick response time—an officer's ability to react effectively in times of danger.

Ratelwacht (*rattlewatch*)—constables armed with loud rattles to warn away lawbreakers.

snitch—a police informer.

swarming—officers overwhelming a suspect by coming at him from different directions simultaneously.

trigger-happy—firing a weapon before determining if it's necessary.

vigorish—petty perks considered a fringe benefit of the job.

War on Drugs—the ongoing effort by police and federal authorities to stamp out the marketing of illegal substances.

whistle-blower—an officer who reveals misbehavior in a police department or by another officer.

INDEX